Lairds, Bards, and Mariners:

The Scot in Northwest America

William Clark

Captain James Cook

Lairds, Bards, and Mariners:

The Scot in Northwest America

by Bruce Le Roy

Foreword by Robert Hitchman

Published for the Washington State American Revolution Bicentennial Commission by the Washington State Historical Society and the Center for Northwest Folklore

Table of Contents

Illustrations

Foreword

Fifteen years ago the Washington State Historical Society started in an organized way to gather material on ethnic history — all sorts of material relating to the various ethnic groups that have come to this part of the world. The Society believed it important to know why these people came, what brought them here and — most important — what special cultural and economic contributions they have made and are making to life in the Pacific Northwest. Under the new director of the Society the project was pursued with enthusiasm.

Ethnic history was the theme of the 1963 Pacific Northwest History Conference sponsored by the Washington State Historical Society and held in Tacoma. Some twenty ethnic groups were represented by the Conference speakers. Talks and discussions were taped for permanent record and undoubtedly the session stimulated new and wide-spread interest in this important aspect of local and regional history.

The Washington State Bicentennial Commission recognized the Society's work in this field and sponsored a series of ethnic histories as one of the state's major bicentennial projects. Bruce Le Roy served as general editor and to date six histories have been published. They are listed in the back of this volume. At the close of the Bicentennial year the Commission made a grant to the Washington State Historical Society to insure a continuation of the project. More histories are in process and it is expected that the series will be continued well into the future.

The task of writing an ethnic history is not an easy one. Primarily such a record is the story of individuals — scores and hundreds of individuals, each bringing his or her talents to a new environment. Leaders emerge from time to time, but what concerns us particularly are the innumerable bits of life and lore and culture the immigrant carries along, folklore and folk arts, customs and traditions, music and art, crafts, work habits and skills, attitudes and wisdom.

In this book Bruce Le Roy melds into separate chapters an overview of the history of some of the Scots who contributed to the history of the Pacific Northwest. Not all Scots could be included in a book of this length. Rather he has chosen to include those whose activities were representative of various occupational groups: the explorers, scientists, fur-traders, mariners, investors, farmers, poets and artists whose total achievements altered northwest history. Here, too, is a generous sampling of the Scottish culture and folklore that has spread through a sort of osmosis to non-Scots here.

Lairds, Bards and Mariners: the Scot in Northwest America can serve as a catalyst for further study and research. Historians may now turn their attention to other individual Scots, Scottish enterprises and achievements. Much more can be done on the aspects of our history and environment that reflect Scottish thinking and tradition.

It is our sincere hope that the present series of ethnic histories will spark continuing concern and scholarly effort in this fascinating and important field.

Robert Hitchman, *President*
Washington State Historical Society

1889 James E. Stuart — Mt. Rainier and mouth of the Puyallup River.

Introduction

"Much may be made of a Scotchman if he be caught young," said Dr. Johnson to James Boswell. Next of Johnson's priorities would be getting out of Scotland: "Sir: the noblest prospect which a Scotchman ever sees is the high-road that carries him to England."[1] Boswell, the young Scot, was silent. What could you ever say to Samuel Johnson when he had his mind made up?

But then Johnson decided to visit Scotland, after considerable urging. William Robertson, Chancellor of Edinburgh University, discussed the forthcoming trip with Boswell: "He sometimes cracks his jokes upon us, but he will find that we can distinguish between the stabs of malevolence and the rebukes of the righteous, which are like excellent oil, and break not the head." Muttered Edmund Burke, when told of the exchange, "Oil, yes," and added, "oil of vitriol."[2]

"To Scotland, however, he ventured; and he returned from it in great good humour, with his prejudices much lessened, and with very grateful feelings of the hospitality with which he was treated, as is evident from that admirable work, his *Journey to the Western Islands of Scotland . . .*" thus reported Boswell, in his own account of the trip with Johnson, *Tour to the Hebrides.*

In 1773, at the time of their visit, the emigration from the Highlands reached what Johnson termed "an epidemical fury." Scots were leaving for North America, Australia, and other parts of the world in great numbers. Poverty, over-population, rising rents, bad harvests, and evictions from the land, called "the Clearances," were the "push factors" which drove them. Add to these "transportation," which meant sending into foreign exile those engaged in rebellious acts against the Crown or who otherwise broke the law. Scotland was being drained of some of its best people.

Dr. Johnson disapproved of all this. When Boswell introduced the subject of emigration, he replied: "To a man of mere animal life you can urge no argument against going to America but that it will be some time before he will get the earth to produce. But a man of any intellectual equipment will not easily go and immerse himself and his posterity for ages in barbarism."[3] Despite his reservations, now, just two years before the outbreak of the American Revolution, the Scots were going, in ever-increasing numbers. Many who had preceded them would be leaders in the Revolution, not finding any discomfort in a battle against the British crown. Boswell commented, "In the morning I walked out and saw the ship, the *Margaret of Clyde,* fairly pass by with a number of emigrants on board. It was a kind of melancholy sight."[4]

While visiting Skye, in the Hebrides, a port from which heavy emigration was occurring, Boswell reported that he and Dr. Johnson "had a good dinner, and in the evening a great dance . . . we performed with much activity a dance which I suppose the emigration from Skye has occasioned. They call it 'America'. A brisk reel is played. The first couple begin, and each sets to one . . . then each to the other . . . then as they set to the next couple, the second and third couples are setting; and so it goes on till all are set a-going, setting and wheeling round each other, while each is making the tour of all in the dance. It shows how emigration catches till all are set afloat. Mrs. Mackinnon told me that the last year when the ship sailed from Portree for America, the people on shore were almost distracted when they saw their relations go off; they lay down on the ground and tumbled, and tore the grass with their teeth. This year there was not a tear shed. The people on shore seemed to think that they would soon follow. This is a mortal sign."[5]

It was "a mortal sign," certain enough. Beginning after the battle of Culloden in 1746, when the clans under Prince Charlie tried for the last time to throw off the English yoke, and lost decisively, the numbers of Scots who left for America began to swell to a mighty flood. Culloden, "that bleak moor, stained with the best blood of Scotland," was to Scotland what Gettysburg would be to the Confederacy in the American Civil War. The high tide crested, broke, and fell.

Then came "the Clearances," when alien land-owners drove out the Highland farmers, "the Clans driven out by an army of sheep" who needed more land for grazing. What the Clearances began was finished by the failure of harvests and the raising of rents. No wonder that the Scot looked toward America for freedom and economic independence. Boswell and Johnson saw the melancholy result of all this turmoil during their visit to Scotland in 1773.

At another point on their tour Boswell reported that "we had a company of thirty at supper, and all was good humour and gaiety. Many songs were sung, one in particular to encourage the emigrants, which had a chorus ending always with 'Tullishale'. (A Gaelic word, *tuillidh seol*, meaning 'more sail', or 'more way', or 'guidance')." The song seems to have been lost, but there were several songs about emigration, its joys, sorrows and consequences, sung not only in Scotland, but abroad. Two are reproduced in a later chapter.[6]

Two years after his trip to the Hebrides with Johnson, Boswell met Captain James Cook who was preparing for his third and last voyage. That voyage would serve to open up the northwest coast of America, spurring Scots to enter the fur trade whose potential riches Cook's published journal would reveal. James Cook's father was a Scot, and the Captain treated Boswell with kindness and tact. Boswell was so impressed by the great navigator that he rushed back to tell Dr. Johnson that he was contemplating signing on for Cook's expedition — one which would lead to the exploration of northwest America, the discovery of the Hawaiian (or Sandwich) Islands, and eventually (without Cook, who was killed in Hawaii), to China.[7] Johnson listened impatiently, then deflated his impulsive friend. Think what might have been! If Boswell's observant mind and ready pen *had* come along on Cook's last voyage, what a classic report might have been born for northwest history, and for world literature.

Well, history is full of ironies and Boswell didn't make the trip. He did manage to demonstrate his esteem for Captain Cook when he presented him with an inscribed copy of his book, *Account of Corsica*. That book is now a treasured possession of the Mitchell Library in Sydney, Australia. Boswell left the book when he visited Captain and Mrs. Cook at their home in Mile End on the outskirts of London. The inscription read: "Presented to Captain Cooke by the Authour, as a small memorial of his admiration of that Gentleman's most renowned merit as a Navigator, of his esteem of the Captain's good sense and worth, and of the grateful sense which he shall ever entertain of the civil and communicative manner in which the Captain was pleased to treat him. James Boswell."[8]

The French historian, Tocqueville, who could not equate equality with liberty, visited America in the 1830's, and in the great book which resulted from the journey, *De la democratie en Amerique*, said: "Not only does democracy make every man forget his ancestors, but it hides his descendants and separates his contemporaries from him; it throws him back forever upon himself alone and threatens in the end to confine him entirely within the solitude of his own heart."[9] What would he say today about America's fascination with "Roots," with her citizens beginning to explore their ethnic beginnings? He was acutely aware of the distinctions of the class system, as practiced in Europe, and of the barriers which birth could make permanent. That an individual could be trapped forever within the confines of one class, without any hope of upward mobility, he also knew. He was resigned to the fact that the solution might be found in migration to the new world — a world of freedom, out from under the ancient restrictions of a society ruled by class, inheritance, or aristocratic custom. In Tocqueville's terms, then, was it any wonder that the citizens of the new world were so quick to put ancestral ties behind them?

Not all of them did, nor were all ties forgotten, as witness the burgeoning of ethnic societies on American soil. For the transplanted Scot there were the Caledonian Society, the St. Andrews Society, or the Robert

Burns clubs. They had their counterparts for just about every other ethnic group which came to America.

In tracing patterns of emigration one finds that people often sought to settle in those regions of America which bore a close resemblance to the home country. Scandinavians found the north woods and sea coasts compatible. Greeks migrated to the Florida keys where warm water fishing and sponge diving did not differ much from the trades in the Aegean islands. Basques came to the dry mountains of the west to herd sheep, as in the Pyrenees. Highland farmers traded the miseries of home for the mountains of the southeastern United States. The Lowland Scot went to tidewater, as he had lived in Galloway or beside the Firth, or in the Orkneys or Shetland islands.

The Scot, Highlander or Lowlander, found the Pacific Northwest, with its rugged mountains, seashore, and, on the coast, rainy, cool climate, a suitable place to settle. Scotland itself, or at least two-thirds of it, has similar conditions of climate and geography. As the most northerly of Great Britain's three countries, Scotland is generally hilly, cool, and, in the west, a wet country which stretches from the Solway Firth and the English border to the Pentland Firth in the north, with the Orkney Islands, Fair Isle, and the Shetland Islands beyond; and, from the North Sea in the east to the Atlantic Islands of the Hebrides and St. Kilda in the west.[10] With great salmon running up northwestern rivers, as in Scotland, and with great ships docking in northwestern ports — many built on the Clyde — the Scot was right at home.

Apparently no one has ever attempted to isolate the story of the Scot from the general history of the Pacific Northwest. Many of the Scottish names which rise to the surface, like McLoughlin, Cook, David Douglas, Alexander Mackenzie, are accepted as almost a part of the natural order. Charlotte Erickson, an author who has made a study of the letters written back to Great Britain by people who emigrated to America, has termed the Scot as one of "the invisible immigrants."[11] As a white, English-speaking settler, the Scot was soon absorbed into the melting pot. Unlike new Americans who came here from other European countries, or from Asia or Africa, he found few problems in eventual acceptance by the Establishment, from the colonial period on. From the 17th century he often became a part of it. Fiercely independent, the Scot soon won personal security in American life. Of course, there were always exceptions.

A clue to the sometimes carefree adaptation to American life was probably due to the life he left behind him. "The sweetest Scottish songs are those of saddest memories." Despite fierce pride in his heritage, the Scot knew that the history of Scotland was one of successive defeats. Wars with England raged through the centuries, wars generally lost. Religious conflicts, such as the battles of the Covenanters with the established church, spurred many to leave Scotland.

Classics of Scottish minstrelsy are filled with epic accounts of the death of heroes: Sir William Wallace, the defeat of Prince Charlie at Culloden, the failure of "the Risings" of 1715 and 1745, lost battles at Dunbar and Flodden Field: It has been said that to tour Scotland today is to pass from one melancholy ruin to another, and that all Scotland retains is "her law, the kirk, and the General Assembly of the Church of Scotland." The memory of an heroic past, a past filled with ruin and disaster, is probably what binds Scots together, no matter in what corner of the globe they live.[12]

In a recent address to Parliament, Queen Elizabeth promised to return a form of self-government to Scotland. The statement startled many Americans who thought that Scotland had been free for centuries. If the promise is kept, the future of Scotland may differ from the record of the past 300 years. Cynical expressions have been heard that this all depends on how much oil is extracted from the offshore fields in the North Sea, off Scotland's coast. Only time will tell.

The ethnic historian walks a path sometimes hedged by brambles of nationalistic pride, suspicion, even racial intolerance. There is no such thing as *best* when considering contributions from different ethnic groups. To draw invidious comparisons is potentially harmful, self-defeating, and a great waste of time. We should be dealing with enlightened appreciation, through an understanding of the changes which take place when an ethnic culture is transplanted from one country to another.

One of the most useful guides was defined by Richard Dorson, a past president of the American Folklore Society and author of several important books. Dorson sees our job as an effort "to compare nationality traditions in the United States with their forms and functions in the lands of their origins."[13] Speaking specifically of the Scot in America, he says the aim is "to contrast Scottish-American with Scottish folk tradition and folk customs." The ethnic historian must deal with "traditional observances, cuisine, demonology, remedies, entertainments." His question is, "what happened to the folkways and folk beliefs after their possessors came to the United States?" His book, *American Folklore and the Historian* lays the ground rules — "the full story of (ethnic) implantation and acculturation can never be told without considering immigrant folk traditions."[14]

Following Dorson's lead, I have tried to include most of the categories he mentioned. For traditional observances, the "Gatherings of the Clan," the Highland Games, Robert Burns nights, and more; for cuisine, start with haggis, move on to cockaliki soup, Scot trifle, and more; of demon-ology, though the Scot brought no beliefs about droll creatures like the Irish leprechaun, or the Norwegian troll, he did fall comfortably into the tradition of the northwest's "Loch Ness monster," the Ogopogo of Lake Okanogan, and of the Sasquatch, or Big Foot, first reported by David Thompson; one also hears some fine ghost stories where transplanted Scots gather together over "a wee drappie." Folk medicine for the Scot is a world in itself, and is dealt with in a later chapter. "Entertainments," in the sense that Dorson uses the word, would include "going St. Andrewing," again the Highland Games, folk dancing, piper's band concerts, Robert Burns nights, the social event of any Scottish club or lodge — and a later chapter tells of a typical one, called "The Cronies." Someone once said that if three Scots were cast away on a desert island which already contained three Englishmen, that no time at all would elapse before the Scots organized "a kirk, a lodge, and a pub," complete with officers, rules and regulations. The English, not being properly introduced, would do no such thing!

Scottish Ambition

"My lady," said David Shand, in Sir James Barrie's play *What Every Woman Knows*, "there are few more impressive sights in the world than a Scotsman on the make!"[15]

Applied to the Scottish emigrant to the United States this may be an understatement. Ambition to succeed in the new world, after the frustra-tions and tragedies of the life he left behind, was a real, driving factor which led to some great success stories. The "canny Scot" was no mis-nomer.

As mentioned earlier, nine, or nearly a quarter of all American Presi-dents were of Scottish descent. [16] (List supplied upon request). Well, since you may never ask, here are the Presidents whose fathers, mothers, or both, carried "Old Scotia" in their veins: James Monroe, the fifth Presi-dent, descended from Andrew Monroe who emigrated to America from Scotland in mid-17th century; James Polk, eleventh in line, was the great-great grandson of Robert Polk (or Pollock), who came from Ayrshire via Ulster to America; James Buchanan, fifteenth President, who was of Ulster Scot parentage; Ulysses S. Grant, a direct descendant from Matthew Grant who came from Scotland to Dorchester, Massachusetts, in 1630; Ruther-ford B. Hayes, nineteenth President, whose ancestor from Scotland settled in Windsor, Connecticut; Chester Arthur, twenty-first President, the son of a Belfast minister of Scottish descent; William McKinley, twenty-fifth President, the descendant of David McKinley, an Ulster Scot and his Ulster Scot wife, Rachel Stewart; Theodore Roosevelt, twenty-sixth President, who was Scotch on his mother's side, Dutch on his father's — she was descended from James Bullock, a Scot who emigrated to Charleston, South Carolina, about 1728; Woodrow Wilson, twenty-eighth in line, whose mother, Janet Woodrow, was the daughter of the Reverend Thomas Woodrow, of Paisley, Scotland.

Scots aiming at the Presidency haven't done too well lately — the latest aspirant being Adlai Stevenson whose grandfather served as Vice-President under Cleveland. Stevenson's Scottish ancestor came from Stirlingshire to America in the 18th century. Five other Scots besides Stevenson served as Vice-Presidents: John C. Calhoun, George Dallas, John Breckenridge, Henry Wilson, Thomas Hendricks, except for Calhoun a veritable "league of forgotten men."

The question of whether or not this kind of nationalistic hornblowing is in good taste seldom bothers a Scot, who, unlike his reticent cousin to the south, releases his frustration this way. So . . . nine of the Signers of the Declaration of Independence were of Scottish descent: Rutledge, Hooper, Ross, Thornton, McKean, Taylor, Wilson, Livingston, and Witherspoon; the first Chief Justice of the United States, John Marshall, whose mother was a Keith; the second Chief Justice, John Rutledge, and two of the first Associate Justices, Blair and Wilson, were of Scottish descent.

Rejoice that I did not list the officers of the American Revolution or the members of the first Continental Congress who were from Scotland or descended from Scots (rebellion against England came quite naturally to men whose families had fled Scotland after the Jacobite risings). Enough is enough!

Where does one find Scottish history and how relate it to the history of the northwest? According to an article in *The American Archivist* which I recommend highly to all interested in writing ethnic history, "most library and archival institutions have *generally chosen not to collect* (italic mine) ethnic materials, due to lack of space, funds, interest, or awareness of the significance of ethnic-related materials."[18] There are exceptions, of course, and with renewed popular interest in "Roots," the situation is starting to improve. The Washington State Historical Society has been gathering material for two decades, and is now working through its Center for Northwest Folklore; Western Reserve Historical Society, in Cleveland; the Ohio Historical Society, in Columbus; the Wisconsin Historical Society, in Madison; the Minnesota Historical Society, in St. Paul, and the Immigration Research Center at the University of Minnesota; the Balch Institute, in Philadelphia; the Folklore Institute, at Indiana University, in Bloomington, and the Folklore Center at UCLA; all of these distinguished institutions are deep in ethnic history, collecting and publishing and making available necessary materials for scholarly research.[19]

I found little help in this study of the Scot in northwest history in the archives of this region. One must ferret out relevant material from published biographies, including the "Mug Book," the popular subscription-sale county histories of the late 19th and early 20th century lists. Looking into diaries, letters and business records of Scottish pioneers, such as the rich resources of fur-trade history, was very helpful. Of course, the primary sources were never catalogued as "Scottish history," so much digging was required. The files of *The Beaver,* the excellent magazine published by the Hudson's Bay Company, were an invaluable resource, as were the book publications of the Hudson's Bay Record Society.[20] The series on the mountain men and fur traders published by the Arthur Clark Company was also useful. The Bibliographical Essay at the end of this book lists other sources, such as the Lewis and Dryden *Marine History of the Pacific Northwest.*

Prologue

He was adventurous or cautious, hard-headed or sentimental, a planner or a dreamer, the "Lord of the streams and forests" or "a Hyporborean nabob." It depended upon who made the appraisal of the Scot in northwest history.Even Washington Irving was sometimes contradictory, and he was himself the son of an Orcadian farmer.[1] To most historians the Scot was an eternal contradiction.

We will examine the Scot in relation to key areas of northwest history. What role did he play in exploration and discovery, the fur trade, maritime history, agriculture, science, politics, commercial investment, literature and art? The picture emerges of an energetic, ambitious, hard-working people who tempered the sobriety of everyday existence with the stuff of adventure and romance. For only as seekers after adventure can we account for many of the Scots who played important roles on the northwest stage.

Part of the romance was in the folklore which he brought with him, "sea-changes" that folklore endured in the shift from Scotland to America. The gathering of such materials is an important task, since it is generally the native traditions and customs which help to distinguish one ethnic group from another. Richard Dorson has said that there must be "the necessary annotation that involves tedious research through glossaries, indexes, field reports, town histories, and any other available sources . . . the field collector knows that his contributions come from speakers, while the 'library collector' can never be sure, without proper documentation, that his author has not invented, improved or adapted from other authors his proverbs, tales and songs."[2]

One cannot separate the Scot from Scottish tradition: the celebration of Robert Burns Night, the Highland Games, the "Border Ballads," or the legends and tales of the "things that go bump in the night." Such folklore is an integral element in the story. Nor can we always accept his own self-appraisals, which may be as misleading as that from George Bryce, the Canadian historian, who boasted that "the world's greatest lyric singer was Robert Burns; the world's greatest novelist, Sir Walter Scott; the two greatest historians, Macaulay and Carlyle."[3] The statement said more about Bryce and the time in which he wrote (1911) than it did about world literature and the Scottish contribution. Shakespeare critics and Tolstoi or Dickens admirers would never agree. As for Macaulay and Carlyle, the school of "great man history' which they represented has long been passed over. Only Winston Churchill followed that guidon in our time, but his work was removed from the mainstream of modern historical literature by a country mile.

Diaries and letters, county and regional histories, and the standard Scottish histories have been consulted in the making of this study. No thematic collections of Scottish source material exist in any Pacific Northwest depository, and there may be none in the United States. Our own Washington State Historical Society, in its Center for Northwest Folklore, has made a beginning, collecting materials for all of the ethnic groups which contributed to regional history.[4] Where possible, people of Scottish birth or descent have been interviewed, originally as a part of the research for this book. There are many more to be recorded.

Several areas of regional ethnic history should be explored, particularly where the Scot is concerned. The Scottish emigration following World War I needs investigation, occurring during the depression of the Thirties. Shipyard after shipyard on the Clyde at Glasgow closed down.[5] Naval architects, engineers and mechanics fled to the shipyards of the Pacific coast, a continuance of the "brain drain" that has plagued Scotland for three centuries. And much can be learned about northwest agriculture, particularly in regard to some of the great farms of eastern Washington which were pioneered and, in some cases, are still owned by Scottish emigrants, or the descendants of emigrants.

Another gap occurs in the lack of a definitive study of the roles of Scottish women in northwest history. Proper credit is given here to Frances Simpson, Susan Moir Allison, and Abigail Scott Duniway, but their biographies are only a small part of the story. That these three women left written records made the task easier, but with certain exceptions, our regional history was written by *men*, and the contributions made by women were generally neglected. Charlotte Erickson called the people who came here from the British Isles "the invisible immigrants."[6] The term certainly applies to Scottish women, though that is not the sense she imputed.

The Scot who emigrated to America was absorbed quickly into the mainstream of American life. Many became leaders in sciences, industry and philanthropy.[7] Scots were never known for their modesty. I remember my first visit to Edinburgh, where my cab driver, elated to learn that he would be the first to introduce me to Scotland, gave me a lecture along the famous "Mile". His subject was Scottish genius and how it had changed world history. He avowed that we owe the telephone, the first steam engine, penicillin, among other things, to Scots.[8] His list was long, and I have forgotten the rest of it. But for this study of Scots in northwest America we do not have to go so far afield as to claim Alexander Hamilton, Patrick Henry or Andrew Carnegie for northwest history, though an argument could be made that what they achieved affected us all. There is a selected list of distinguished Scots in the Appendix, enough to show that the Scottish contribution to our regional history was nearly incalculable. More names could have been added, in a foredoomed effort to please everybody, but we had to stop somewhere.

The search began with my first trip to Scotland in 1961, followed by a second in 1970, and led to Beaver House,[9] then the world headquarters of the venerable Hudson's Bay Company which dispatched so many Scots to the Pacific Northwest; to the British Museum, where the journals of several key figures are archived;[10] to the East-West Center, of the University of Hawaii, and the Hawaiian Historical Society, with their wonderful collections of early voyages to the Northwest Coast, and on David Douglas' tragic story; to the libraries of Harvard, Yale, California, and Washington; to half a dozen American historical societies; finally, to help from the innumerable friends and colleagues who took an interest in this quest for Scottish "Roots".

As Bishop Percy quoted in his *Reliques*, "All Scotland thither came . . such an host of that nation was never seen before; their names were numbered to nine score thousands, truly by their owne tunge, as it was told after." He was talking about an historic battle, but it almost seems to apply to our story of Scottish emigration to northwest America. Not *quite* "nine score thousand" were used in the writing of this study — it only seems that way, but here there are more than enough "lairds, bards and mariners" to symbolize them all. Knowing these, perhaps we learn something about them all.[11]

Finally, let us give some credit where credit has long been overdue. Two events, more than any others, served to open the Pacific Northwest to exploration, exploitation and development: Captain James Cook's third voyage, in 1778, and the Lewis and Clark Expedition, 1804-1806. Cook's expedition opened the Northwest to exploration by sea; Lewis and Clark's expedition by land, the transcontinental crossing. That "great English mariner", James Cook, was the son of a Scottish farmer who moved south to England just a few years before James' birth;[13] William Clark, co-captain of the Lewis and Clark Expedition, shared the same Scottish descent as his brother, George Rogers Clark. Most writers mention the older brother's heritage, few ever attribute the same to William!

Washington Irving became identified in the popular mind with a kind of hazy relationship to the Catskill Dutch who fathered Rip Van Winkle. But the author of *Astoria* and the *Adventures of Captain Bonneville* was really the son of a Scottish farmer who emigrated from the Orkney Islands to the United States. In art, we have the man who painted magnificent pictures of the northwest — James E. Stuart.[14] He shared the Scottish background of his uncle, Gilbert Stuart, who was famed for portraits of the founding fathers of the Republic. There were others less well-known.

Apparently the Scots never had a good publicist. This little book may help to balance the equation. "A lazy cat makes a proud mouse" says an old Scottish proverb. Having "chased the cheese" this far, let's move along. It's a great story.

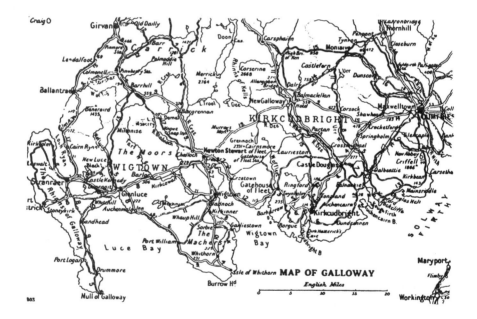

MAP OF GALLOWAY

English Miles

Chapter One

A Journey Home

MACDONALD

One bright June day in 1961, on my first trip to Scotland, I crossed over an old footbridge spanning the River Cree between Minnigaff and Newton Stewart. Passing an abandoned stone woolen mill that sat on the river bank, I began the climb which would take me "Round the Risk", which term, according to the villagers, was traditional to describe the ascent to the site of the ruins of "Risk Castle" where my mother's people had lived until the end of the 17th century. This was the Murdock family, a sept of Clan Donald.[1]

Beyond the bridge the path wound past the old Kirk of Minnigaff, skirting an ancient cemetery, some of whose stones bore family names. From here the road wound upward between stone "dykes" or fences which bordered the path and enclosed the rolling lands of Cumloden. As I climbed I could look down across the fields where white fallow deer were grazing. Fields and deer were now the property of the Earl of Galloway whose ancestors had acquired Cumloden after the Murdock family left for America.[2] Birds tumbled and sang in the bright air as I climbed. No telephone wires marred the rustic view, nor were any people or cars in sight. Wild roses climbed over the dykes by the roadside, and the fields were full of blooming wildflowers. Probably the view had changed little since Robert Murdock sailed for America in 1687.[3]

In the *History of the Lands and their Owners in Galloway*, P. H. McKerlie described Cumloden, invoking its spell in a poetic way: "The main family is now out of Galloway, as the foregoing will show, but the name is still to be found in the district, and doubtless from offshoots of the Cumloden family. The old residence was about two miles from the church of Minnigaff, close to the water of Penkill, and, in the seventeenth century, is mentioned as a good house situated in a wood with orchards. It is known as Risk Castle, and is on the farm of that name, but little more than the site now remains. The ruins are nearly on a level with the ground, and mostly covered with turf, the materials having been carted to build the dykes and the new farmhouses. A small shed has recently been erected on the site with some of the materials. The castle does not appear to have been large from the site . . . the situation is very beautiful, being in a small wood surrounded with parks near the head of the glen, with Penkill Burn close by murmuring on its course. It is surrounded with hills, being near to the base of the Garlic on the north side, and Stronnbac on the east."[4]

This is historic country, the setting for novels by Sir Walter Scott, Robert Louis Stevenson, Sir James Barrie, and John Buchan. In *Tales of a Grandfather* Scott tells how Robert the Bruce was chased into the highlands of Galloway by pursuing English troops. Three brothers, Murdock of

Cumloden, Mackie of Larg, and McClurg of Kirrouchtree, fought by his side. They stood by him through a long, discouraging campaign until final victory at Bannockburn. Robert wanted to reward his faithful allies, but the brothers asked permission to refer the question to their mother. The old lady told the King that she would like "the wee bit hassock atween Palnure and Penkill" to be awarded to her valiant sons. "The wee bit hassock" formed a triangle with a base of three miles along the River Cree, and extended five miles back into the interior.[5]

The King granted her request and the land was divided among the three sons. The King also granted them arms, those of Murdock, as recorded in the Lyon Register, being "two ravens hanging pale-ways, sable, with an arrow through both their heads, proper." His crest was "a raven rising, sable, having an arrow thrust through his heart, headed and feathered, argent. Motto—*Omnia pro bono*" (or, "all for good"). The arms memorialized an archery contest when the three youths demonstrated their prowess before the king. The Murdock Coat of Arms is reproduced in this book.[6]

Two small stones from Risk Castle weight a pile of manuscript beside me as I write. They were recovered from the ruins of the castle when I visited Scotland again in 1970. We had just come from Beaver House, in London, where we were a part of a delegation from the Washington State Historical Society which had come over for a memorable joint celebration of the 300th anniversary of the Hudson's Bay Company.[7] The Company practically controlled the Pacific Northwest for three decades in the early 19th century. The archives in London showed that "The Company of Adventurers trading into Hudson's Bay" included many Scots among the key people who guided her destinies for three centuries. Now, in Scotland once more, my family and I visited Cumloden, where we were entertained with great courtesy by the Earl of Galloway and his charming Lady.

Over tea in the drawing room of the lovely old manor house, the Earl regaled us with interesting local history. Knowing that I had just been appointed chairman of Washington State's forthcoming participation in the bicentennial of the American Revolution, the Earl was reminded of a local figure who had left Galloway. This individual had gone on to "achieve a measure of success." Measure of success, indeed! He was referring to John Paul Jones, the father of the American Navy.

Not far from Cumloden, near Kircudbright (pronounced "Kir-coo-brie") on St. Mary's Isle, is the ancestral home of the Earl of Selkirk. It was here that John Paul (he took the name "Jones" later) was raised.[8] His father served as a gardener for the fourth Earl of Selkirk. At the age of twelve, the lad was apprenticed to one John Younger, a Kircudbright shipper, and sailed as a cabin boy to Virginia. When the Younger firm failed, John Paul was released from his apprenticeship, becoming a crew member on a Jamaican slaver-brigantine. The chief mate died during the voyage and he was appointed to his place, following which the Captain also died at sea, and it was left to young John Paul to bring the ship safely home to port. His reward was an appointment as master of the ship. Not long after, he purchased his own ship and made a number of voyages in the Tobago trade.

Through his brother who had preceded him to America and had settled in Virginia, John Paul met a number of southern leaders in the burgeoning revolutionary movement. In the autumn of 1775, acting upon the advice of Joseph Hewes, a member of the Continental Congress, he went to Philadelphia where he was commissioned a senior lieutenant in the newly formed Continental navy. From this point on, his naval exploits became legendary.

In 1778, on one of his now famous raiding expeditions, he was cruising through St. George's channel and the Irish Sea. There he took a number of naval prizes. On April 23, 1778, with 31 volunteers, he went ashore at Whitehaven, a British stronghold. Here he spiked the cannon at two British fortifications. The same day, at noon, he landed at St. Mary's Isle, on the coast of Scotland, and his old home. He had an audacious plan. He would seize his father's old employer, the Earl of Selkirk, hoping to use him as a pawn in negotiating with the British over the release of American prisoners of war. (The tale has strange similarities to the flight of Nazi leader, Rudolph Hess, into Scotland during World War II, where he attempted unsuccessfully to get the Duke of Hamilton to negotiate the end of fighting between Great Britain and Germany, enabling both nations to cooperate in the defeat of the Soviet Union. Hess was not as fortunate as John Paul Jones. He has been a prisoner of the Allies from that day to this, spending nearly forty years in solitary exile).

When Jones landed at St. Mary's Isle he learned that the Earl of Selkirk was away on business, so he had to be content with polite conversation. While their commander was thus preoccupied, the landing-party went about the manor house, "liberating" the family silver, gorgeous ancestral plates engraved with vignettes from the history of the ancient family.[9] Upon returning to the ship, Jones learned what the crew had done. He was furious, feeling that the act had been a breach of etiquette, if not of the Articles of War which permitted the taking of loot on enemy soil. He sent a local boy back to the estate bearing a note in which he pledged to redeem the silver and to arrange for its return. He kept the promise, using the offices of his good friend, Benjamin Franklin, who was Minister to

France. The action precipitated a grateful correspondence from the Earl of Selkirk. Not only did he write to Jones, chiding him for thinking he was important enough to affect the course of the war, or for thinking that he had any influence whatever with the British government, but thanking him still for his gentlemanly behavior to Lady Selkirk, and for the restrained actions of the crew while on St. Mary's Isle. But he also wrote to the mighty *Times* of London, a thing Englishmen of quality frequently do when deeply moved. In his letter to the *Times,* Selkirk took issue with those critics who were calling Jones "that bloody pirate" who raided his former homeland. Instead he saluted him as a man of his word and a naval gentleman.[10]

During Jones' raid on St. Mary's Isle he was closely observed by the boy who would one day become the fifth Earl of Selkirk. He would also become Governor of the Hudson's Bay Company. The lad was deeply impressed by the Commodore's courtesy, and also by his promise to redeem the family silver and to restore it to its rightful owners, a vow he kept faithfully. In his mature years, the fifth Earl is reputed to have commented upon the character of John Paul Jones as a kind of model of "the new man" to be found in America. Years later, as Governor of the Hudson's Bay Company, the Earl arranged to finance a mass migration of Scottish farmers to the Red River colony in North America.[11] His belief that greater opportunity for self-betterment existed in America, for the depressed yeoman-farmers struggling for a hard-scrabble living in Scotland, motivated his generous action.

A few years after the Scottish emigration to the Red River, and, as part of an effort to help counter the growing American infiltration into the Oregon country, a large party of Red River colonists made their way down to Puget Sound.[12] Some went further, to the Willamette Valley. The Puget Sound party aimed for Fort Nisqually, then a stronghold for the Hudson's Bay Company although it was rapidly becoming an island in a spreading sea of American expansionism. Today, the descendants of a number of the original Red River migration call this area home, living still in Tacoma, Roy, Seattle, and surrounding areas. The Ross family, the Murray family, the Flett family, are a few of the names involved.[13] It may be too much to say that they are here today because John Paul Jones kept his promise to Lord and Lady Selkirk! But the impression he left upon the young Earl-to-be was certainly one factor in the attitude of later years which could see new life for fellow Scots in America. Perhaps, too, the youthful experience was one motivation years later when he encouraged and financed their emigration to the Red River colony.

Theorizing aside, the visit to Cumloden and the interesting conversation with the Earl of Galloway, brought home most forcefully the strangely intimate ties one finds between an ancient castle in Scotland and the history of our own Pacific Northwest. Because so many of the people who helped create our early history came here from Scotland, it would probably be possible to find counterpart stories wherever one goes in Scotland today.

The story of Captain Sir William Drummond Stewart, of Grandtully, would be another addition to the canon.[14] A Scottish sportsman, visiting the American west just for the devilish adventure of it all, Stewart was present when the party of missionaries arrived at rendezvous on the Green River. Narcissa Whitman and Eliza Spaulding were the first white women to make the transcontinental crossing, and they charmed the itinerant Scot. He was accompanied by a young artist, Alfred Jacob Miller, whose record of their experiences is one of the great artistic treasures of western history. Though reproduced elsewhere, one way to appreciate Miller's work is to examine those paintings and sketches which Bernard De Voto used in his classic *Across the Wide Missouri*.[15]

Stewart's method was to attach himself to one of the fur trade parties which were criss-crossing the Rockies and the further west during the early nineteenth century. It was most effective, and we find him with Nathaniel Wyeth, in Oregon, not long after meeting the Whitman-Spalding party at the fur-trade rendezvous on the Green River, a thousand miles to the east. One of his experiences was a visit to Dr. John McLoughlin at Fort Vancouver, joining that venerable figure at great dinners while a Scottish piper circled the table, playing softly for the delectation of the guests. A typical dinner at Fort Vancouver might consist of roast beef, elk steaks, ham raised and cured on the Company farm, a variety of vegetables, and dessert, perhaps apple duff delicately flavored with spices. Stewart could not have dined better at one of his friend's castles back home. Or his own, for that matter. (Murthly Castle would become an unusual show place when Stewart finally returned to Scotland.)

Stewart was a veteran of the Battle of Waterloo, and life after the Napoleonic wars seemed too dull for a man cut to his mold. He traveled and hunted in Turkey and Russia, took part in London's social life, and visited Italy and Portugal. Then, when his brother John inherited title to the family estate, they quarrelled and William, swearing he would never sleep under the roof of Murthly Castle as long as John was master, made hasty plans for a hunting trip to western America. He wrote to a number of fellow Scots who were in high positions with the Hudson's Bay Company, including the Governor, Sir George Simpson. The blanket introduction stood him in good stead when he arrived finally in America.

6

By the time he returned home, his brother John was dead and William inherited the estate as next in line. He took two Indians and a half-breed back to Scotland with him. In addition, he had shipped home boxes filled with plants, seeds, animal skins and other memorabilia of his long sojourn in western America. Seedling trees were planted on the castle grounds. Not long after, he sent for Alfred Jacob Miller, the young American artist who had accompanied him on his western travels. Miller brought the sketches he had made, which is what he always called what were really water colors. When settled in, he used the "sketches" as models for some huge paintings of the scenes he had captured while in the West. Among them was the famous painting "The Trapper's Bride," with the figures almost life size. It was so popular, that he made a number of copies of it for admiring visitors.[16]

Eventually, Murthly Castle grounds housed a paddock where Captain Stewart kept a number of buffalo he had shipped home from the west, some American deer, and a number of varieties of western game birds. Murthly Castle became a kind of museum of western "culture" and the mecca for hordes of curious Scots. For years after his return home, Stewart kept up a friendly correspondence with the mountain men and fur-trade managers he had met in the west. Notable among these were Robert Campbell and the Sublettes, who operated out of St. Louis. For several years the Sublettes continued to supply Murthly Castle with new additions for the paddock and the grounds. One letter complained, that even at two hundred a head, live buffalo were hard to come by. Even so, they managed to ship new ones and some replacements from time to time.[17]

Life in Scotland began to pall again, and Stewart returned to western America for one last excursion. This time he intended that his expedition would make real contributions to science. By advance correspondence he arranged to pick up three botanists in St. Louis, two from Germany, and one, Alexander Gordon, from Scotland. John James Audubon, now world famous, was also in St. Louis, and Stewart tried to induce him to join their party. Audubon had already made arrangements to go with an American Fur Company boat, so he could not accept. Lieutenant John Charles Fremont was also organizing his expedition to Oregon, so Stewart offered to join forces, but Fremont planned to take a southern route, so refused.

Two young men whose family connections to western history were impeccable asked to join the expedition. They were Jefferson Clark, the son of Captain William Clark, of the famed Lewis and Clark Expedition, and Captain Clark's nephew, Clark Kennerly. Sir William Drummond Stewart added their names to his roster. And, at the request of Father Pierre-Jean de Smet, Stewart also took along a missionary party which included two priests and two lay helpers. They would travel only as far as St. Mary's Mission among the Flathead Indians, serving as reinforcements for the small group already there. When the party at last headed west William Sublette described it in his journal: "Some of the Armey. Some professional gentlemen. Some on a trip for pleasure. Some for health . . . so we have Doctors, Lawyers, botanists, Bugg Ketchers, Hunters and men of nearly all professions . . ."

The luxurious equipment, including a huge crimson tent for Stewart, and various exotic accoutrements, are all described in *Scotsman in Buckskin*, by Porter and Davenport, the best available life of the adventurous Stewart. It is doubtful that his exploits added anything substantial to western history, excluding the fine art of Alfred Jacob Miller. But he certainly added color!

Earl of Selkirk

John Paul Jones

Chapter Two

From the heather to the sea

THE SHIELDS OF BRUCE AND DOUGLAS

The third voyage of Captain James Cook is celebrated as perhaps the most influential in northwest maritime annals insofar as it set in motion the world trade in furs which would open the northwest to exploration and development.

Almost everyone thinks of Cook as a great English navigator—and he was. But he was also a Scot, the son of a Lowland Scots laborer who crossed the border from Roxburghshire into England, seeking employment in the depressed period following the Jacobite Rebellion of 1715. On his father's side, his grandparents were John Cook, a native of the parish of Ednam, and Jean Duncan, of the parish of Smaillhome. James Cook's mother was Grace Pace, of Yorkshire, and he was born in Marton, Yorkshire, on October 27th, 1728. Scotland and England may both share credit for his sturdy heritage.

1978 marks the bicentennial of Cook's arrival off the Northwest Coast. Two hundred years ago England and America were at war when Cook set sail on what was to be his final voyage. But the Revolution had little to do with his mission, this expedition being planned as one for the purpose of scientific discovery. Benjamin Franklin, then Minister Plenipotentiary to the court of France, representing the new young nation, was deeply concerned that hostilities between the two nations not get in the way of Cook's mission. In a letter to "All Captains and Commanders of armed Ships acting by Commission from the Congress of the United States of America now in War with Great Britain", Franklin pointed out that Cook's undertaking was aimed at "the Increase of Geographical Knowledge . . . facilitates the Communication between distant nations, in the exchange of useful Products and Manufactures and the extension of Arts, whereby the common enjoyments of human life are multiplied and augmented and Science of other kinds increased to the benefit of mankind in general . . . that you would treat the said Captain Cook and his people with all civility and kindness affording them as common friends to mankind all the Assistance in your power which they may happen to stand in need of . . ."[2]

James Cook's contributions to the world and his influence upon the opening of the Pacific Northwest are so well known that it would be superfluous to recount them in this limited study. His three great voyages changed world history, opened countries and continents to settlement and development, leading to the creation of new industries, such as whaling in the South Pacific and the fur-trade on the northwest coast of America. Genius is always a mystery. The son of a Scottish day-laborer and a Yorkshire village woman was an excellent exemplar, though being the right man in the right place at the right time may have helped.

Cook was the first of three men who altered northwest history to die in Hawaii. His death in a skirmish with natives at Kealakekua Bay upon his return from the northwest coast was an unnecessary tragedy.[3] Another important figure in our regional history was Captain John Kendrick, a Massachusetts mariner who sailed together with Captain Robert Gray to the Pacific Northwest in the fur trade. The first American ships in these waters, the *Columbia*, under Gray, and the *Lady Washington*, under Kendrick, were trading off the northwest coast only a few years after Cook first explored the region.

As was customary with those in the Northwest-Hawaii-China trade, Kendrick worked the northwest coast during the summer months, then wintered in the Sandwich Islands (Hawaii). When he brought his ship into Honolulu harbor, a passing ship commanded by Captain William Brown saluted him. A misfired cannon ball struck and killed him.[4] Unlike Gray, whose discovery of the Columbia River helped set the later American claim to the Oregon country, Kendrick's major monument was for self-promotion. His lengthy engagement in questionable real estate deals with the northwest Indians led to claims upon Congress by his survivors which went on for years.[5] Kendrick, I hasten to point out, was no Scot!

The third historic person to die in the Sandwich or Hawaiian Islands was Scottish botanist David Douglas. His story is told in another chapter and it is only the coincidental matter of his death that concerns us here. After three trips to the northwest where he collected thousands of specimens for the Royal Horticultural Society in England, Douglas visited Hawaii for the last time. On a collecting expedition on the slopes of Moana Loa, the volcano on the "Big Island", Douglas fell into a pit which had trapped a wild steer. He was gored to death, another tragic loss to world science.[6]

What does this all mean—see Hawaii and die? No, it is just that the three men, their connections with our history, and their tragic ends in Hawaii, are too coincidental not to mention.

No one ever tried to elevate John Nicol to the same Pantheon where we place his fellow Scot, Captain James Cook. Excepting Cook's journals, however, *The Life and Adventures of John Nicol, Mariner* gives us the narrative of one of the earliest recorded Scottish visitors to the northwest coast.[7] Nicol came as a member of the crew of the *King George*, Captain Nathaniel Portlock commanding. Both Portlock and his fellow commander, George Dixon, had served as navigators on Cook's third voyage. Together they sailed from England in 1785, Dixon commanding the *Queen Charlotte*, and Portlock as captain of the *King George*.

John Nicol had already served in the American Revolution, "taking convoy and capturing American privateers." He had also sailed before under Portlock, noting as he signed on with the *King George*, that his commander would be "my old officer, Lieutenant Portlock, now captain." He does not say where or under what circumstances the prior service was performed. He does say that "he was happy to see me, as I was an excellent brewer of spruce beer, and the very man he wished." Engaged as ship's cooper, Nicol not only knew how to build good barrels and casks, but also knew how to fill them with the potent remedy against the dreaded scurvy which decimated so many ships' crews in the 18th century.

Nicol's narrative is one of the sprightliest accounts of any of the men who visited the northwest coast in the decade following the death of Captain Cook. Enroute to the northwest, the ship hove to off "Owhyee" (now known as Hawaii, the "Big Island"). ". . . . we bore away for the Sandwich Islands. The first land we made was Owhyee, the island where Captain Cook was killed. The *King George* and the *Queen Charlotte* were the first ships which had touched there since that melancholy event. The natives came on board in crowds, and were happy to see us; they recognized Portlock and others who had been on the island before, along with Cook."

Nicol describes the merriment as the crews consorted with the native girls. Social relations resumed at about the point where Cook's crew left off when they retired from the islands in 1779. He tells how the girls came aboard (the captain was afraid to put ashore, fearing a repetition of the events which led to Cook's tragedy), had the run of the ship, and soon formed attachments to members of the crew. There was the gunner's native girl-friend: "the fattest woman I ever saw in my life," said Nicol. "We were forced to hoist her on board; her thighs were as thick as my waist; no hammock in the ship would hold her; many jokes were cracked upon the pair."

Soon after casting anchor, "we had the chief on board who killed Captain Cook — for more than three weeks. He was in bad health, and had a smelling bottle, with a few drops in it, which he used to smell at; we kept it filled for him. There were a good many bayonets in possession of the natives, which they had obtained at the murder of Cook." Portlock and Dixon were anxious to avoid clashes which might end in a tragedy such as befell Cook and his crew. This explains their hospitality to the very people who had been in the skirmish on the beach just six years earlier. There was no attempt to seek revenge upon the natives, only an obvious effort at pacification.

When Nicol arrived at Nootka Sound with Portlock he entered "a swirl of the nations." Ships from several different European countries were trading for the sea otter skins which Cook's published journals had revealed were so plentiful on the northwest coast, and which his crew had found to be of great commercial value on the Canton market. In

1786, the year of their arrival at Nootka, a French expedition, under the Comte de La Perouse, visited there on a voyage of scientific discovery.[9] Captain James Strange, sailing from Bombay, was trading in the area on behalf of the East India Company.[10] Arriving in June, just a month before Portlock's arrival, Strange had sailed north after obtaining some six hundred sea otter skins in trade with the Indians.

But the person who would make an immediate noise on the world stage was Captain John Meares, who, like Strange, had been sent out of India by a group of merchants. Meares' two ships, the *Felice Adventurer* and the *Iphigenia*, were flying the Portugese flag in an attempt to escape paying tribute to the English monopoly. When Meares reached Nootka, however, he erected a post from which he flew the British flag. He went to work collecting furs, built the first vessel, the *Northwest America*, to be launched in northern waters, made several important discoveries, and explored the Strait of Juan de Fuca.

Two years after they met at Nootka, Meares precipitated what would become known as the Nootka Sound Controversy. In 1788 he tried to establish a permanent settlement at Nootka and to set up a monopoly of the fur trade. For the purpose he recruited Captain James Colnett, of the *Argonaut*, and Captain Hudson, of the *Princess Royal*, to join him in the enterprise. But the Spanish viceroy in Mexico City, claiming Spanish dominion, dispatched two ships northward, Captains Martinez and Haro commanding, with instructions to occupy Nootka and to enforce Spanish rights in the region. Thus, when Meares' colleagues Colnett and Hudson arrived, their ships were seized and the two captains and their crews were sent south to San Blas as prisoners.[11]

The confrontation brought Spain and England to the brink of war, in the famed "Nootka Sound Controversy." But the Nootka Convention, signed on October 28, 1790 by Spain and England, brought the sabre-rattling to an end. By terms of the Convention, mutual occupation of Nootka by both nations would be permitted, and war was averted. From that time onward, Spanish influence in the Pacific Northwest declined.[12] Spain surrendered the primacy which she had jealously guarded ever since the papal bull of Pope Alexander had permitted her to consider the Pacific Ocean as "a Spanish lake." As Spain gradually withdrew from the Pacific Northwest, England assumed an authority in the area which would last for the next half century.

But when John Nicol first met Captain Meares the Nootka controversy was still two years in the future. Nicol's narrative foreshadows Meares' propensity for sharp dealing and conspiracy.

"While in Prince William's Sound, the boat went on an excursion to

Snug Harbor Cove, at the top of the Sound. She discovered the *Nootka,*
Captain Mairs (sic), in a most distressing situation from the scurvy.
There were only the captain and two men free from the disease. Two-
and-twenty Lascars had died through the course of the winter; they had
caused their own distress, by their inordinate use of spirits on Christmas
eve. They could not bury their own dead; they were only dragged a
short distance from the ship, and left upon the ice. They had muskets
fixed upon the capstan, and man-ropes that went down to the cabin, that
when any of the natives attempted to come on board, they might fire
them off to scare them . . . (before they began to trade) Captain Mairs
(sic) lowered from the window his barter, and in the same way received
their furs. *The Beaver,* the *Nootka's* consort, had been cut off in the beginning of the winter, and none of her people were ever heard of. We
gave him every assistance in our power in spruce and molasses (Ed. note:
to counteract the scurvy), and two of our crew to assist in working the
vessel, Dickson and George Willis, who stopped at Canton until we arrived; then wishing him well, took our leave of him. Captain Portlock
could have made a fair prize of him, as he had no charter, and was
trading in our limits; but he was satisfied with his bond not to trade on
our coast; but the bond was forfeit as soon as we sailed, and he was in
China before us."

After his cruise with Portlock, Nicol never again returned to the
northwest. Only a brief passage in the entire narrative, his vivid descriptions of the fur trade, native life, and the rugged coast are some of our
best insights for the adventuresome Scots who sailed the seven seas and
played a role in northwest history. The sub-title of *The Life and Adventures of John Nicol, Mariner* is itself a sweeping description of a crowded
career, but it would not be atypical for many of his countrymen. It reads:
"His Service in King's Ships in War & Peace, His Travels & Explorations
by Sea to remote and unknown countries in Merchant Vessels, Whalers,
and other Sundry Craft; together with copious Notes & Comments on
Ships, the Officers and Shipmates with whom he served, the Customs &
Traditions of the Sea and of the Inhabitants of Distant Lands both Savage
and Civilized, their Religions, Culture, & Industries, etc. etc. etc. . . . As
Related by Himself."

When Nicol finally swallowed the anchor and settled in Edinburgh,
he recalled and compared his native land with the far-flung corners of
the world:

". . . and I proceeded to Scotland, determined to settle . . . I arrived in Edinburgh just twenty-five years after I had left it to wander the
globe. I had been only twice there, once at the end of the American war,

when I found my father dead, and my brothers wanderers. After my return from the voyage with Captain Portlock, I remained only a few days, and just passed through the city. When in the *Edgar*, I never had been on shore. I scarce knew a face in Edinburgh. It had doubled itself in my absence. I now wandered in elegant streets where I had left corn growing; everything was new to me. I confess, I felt more sincere pleasure and enjoyment in beholding the beauties of Edinburgh, than ever I felt in any foreign clime, for I now could identify myself with them. I was a Scotchman, and I felt as if they were my own property. In China, in Naples, in Rio Janeiro, or even in London, I felt as a stranger, and I beheld with only the eye of curiosity. Here I now looked on with the eye of a son, who is witnessing the improvements of his father's house."

In disputation with fellow Scots his world experience stood him in good stead: "I bothered them with latitudes and longitudes . . . when they spoke of heavy taxes, I talked of China; when they complained of hard times, I told them of the West India slaves."

John Nicol's *Envoi* was beautiful, sharing the feeling of his fellow Scot, Robert Louis Stevenson, who wrote as an epitaph "Home is the Sailor": "I have been a wanderer, and the child of chance, all my days; and now only look for the time when I shall enter my last ship, and be anchored with a green turf on my breast; and I shall care not how soon the command is given."[13]

Nicol's autobiography was a best-seller in his time and after, possibly serving as an incentive to some of the Scots who emigrated to America. Adventure-seekers who came to work for the Hudson's Bay Company, or for the North West Company, in the rich fur grounds of the west may have been spurred by Nicol's exciting account.

But the real importance of Nicol's book, at least for our purposes, is as a *symbol*, representing all of the young Scots who left the land of the heather to follow the sea. He was no James Cook, no leader of men, nor one to change world geography. He was only a common sailor who still had the eloquence to leave a memorable testament.

Scots have been a seafaring people throughout history, perhaps a legacy from the Norsemen who invaded Scotland from the 9th century onward, mingling blood and cultures. The Shetland and Orkney islands were occupied early after the beginning of the Viking raids. The islands were used as bases for raids and invasions, in England, Wales and Ireland. The clans of northern Scotland became a mixture of Pictish, Scottish (or Celtic), and Scandinavian (or Viking) ancestry.[14]

Sea-girt, Scotland has always looked to the sea for part of its livelihood. Fishermen make their living off the coast of Scotland every year, and Scots have followed the sea for generations. The Scots are also noted shipbuilders. When the Clyde River, near Glasgow, was dredged and deepened for shipping, it became the center for shipbuilding. "Clyde-built" ships became famous around the world during the 19th century. Scottish engineers developed some of the earliest steam-powered vessels there. By the end of 1823 Scotland had built 95 steamships, of which 72 were constructed in Clyde shipyards.[15]

But the Clyde was famous not only for steam. The magnificent *Cutty Sark* was constructed at Dumbarton shipyards in 1868; the *Falls of Clyde* was built in 1878 at Fort Glasgow. Today, the *Cutty Sark* is a floating museum at Greenwich, in England, where it was visited by members of the Washington State Historical Society in 1970 when they came to help celebrate the 300th anniversary of the Hudson's Bay Company. The *Falls of Clyde* is docked on the Honolulu waterfront and is maintained as an adjunct to Hawaii's Bishop Museum.

Some of the most famous passenger liners ever built were created at Clyde shipyards. They include the *Lusitania* (1907); *Acquitania* (1914); the *Queen Mary* (1934); the *Queen Elizabeth* (1938); the *Queen Elizabeth II* (1969). Many naval ships, cargo ships, oil rigs, tankers, channel ships and yachts continue to be built on the Clyde.[16]

Recently, when speaking to about 250 people at an award dinner of the Puget Sound Maritime Historical Society, in Seattle, I asked how many in the audience, all of whom had a maritime background, were of Scottish descent. More than one-half of the crowd raised their hands! Many of the Scots who were trained in Clyde shipyards made their way eventually to the Pacific Northwest. Some were (and are) employed at Bremerton, where ships for the U.S. Navy were built during both world wars. Others were (and are) in commercial shipyards in Seattle and Tacoma.

The best source for indications of Scottish involvement with the maritime trades in the Pacific Northwest is Lewis & Dryden's *Marine History of the Pacific Northwest*. Published in 1895, the book is an absolute treasure of biographical information about the men who sailed these waters from the earliest day of the northwest fur trade. Going through the rolls one finds the men from Scotland divided between the ships' captains and officers and the ships' engineers. Many of these engineers trained at Glasgow on the Clyde.

There being no point in repeating the biographical information available in Lewis & Dryden, I will only list a few of the more interesting careers of transplanted Scots in the maritime: Captain William Irving, born in Annan, Dumfrieshire, Scotland, in 1816, who played an important role in the establishment of steam navigation on the Columbia and Willamette rivers, later in British Columbia; Alexander Sinclair Murray, born in Scotland in 1827, whose career spanned the California gold rush, the Sydney-San Francisco run, and the Fraser River gold rush, in British Columbia; the first steamer built in western Canada; finally, pioneer navigation in Australia and New Zealand;[17] Captain Eugene Thurslow of Seattle, one of the last men to pilot the *Beaver,* venerable Hudson's Bay Company steam boat and the first steamboat to navigate the North Pacific.[18]

Two ships famed in the maritime history of the Pacific Northwest returned to Puget Sound not long ago. The first was a replica of *The Beaver,* reconstructed to honor the history of the 300 year old Hudson's Bay Company.[19] Her crew, recruited in England and Scotland, had several names on her roster which betrayed Scottish descent. The second ship had never been in the northwest in her days of sailing. But the *Nonsuch* was the first ship dispatched to the New World by the Company of Adventurers Trading out of Hudson's Bay. Only 37 feet long on the keel, which meant that her hull was about 50 feet long overall, the *Nonsuch* was 15 feet wide, with a burden of 40 to 50 tons. She generally carried a crew of 12 men, but this was increased to 24 in wartime. Normally she carried six small guns, but the number could be increased to eight. It was a tiny ship for such a great voyage, but she was not considered exceptionally small for a deep-sea merchant ship in the late 17th century.

The *Nonsuch* sailed from the Thames in 1668, with orders to "sail to Hudson Bay by the Northward or Westward according to your owne discretion." She was to anchor in the Bay, set up a fort on land and trade with the Indians. Her orders also called for her return home before ice closed Hudson Strait. She made the Atlantic crossing in 44 days. (This compares with the average 42 day crossing made by the large cargo emigrant-carrying sailing ships all through the 19th century — excellent time for comparative purposes). Her total voyage lasted about 15 months, and though her cargo did not pay for the cost of the voyage, it had proved beyond doubt that direct access by sea to the furs of America was practical.[20]

A beautiful replica of the *Nonsuch* was constructed from original plans and, in 1970, the ship visited Puget Sound. Members of the Washington State Historical Society were delighted guests aboard for a cruise of Commencement Bay. Captain Adrian Small, every inch a British sailor of the old school, gave them a good run, on a cloudy day, with rain and high waves to impart a feeling of history relived.

On May 2, 1670, the group of courtiers and business men who had backed the first trip of the *Nonsuch* received their charter as "The Governor and Company of Adventurers of England trading into Hudson's Bay." The Charter made the Company "the true and absolute Lordes and Proprietors" of about 1,400,000 square miles of North America. 300 years later, to the day, a delegation from the Washington State Historical Society met with the Governor, Lord Amory, and officers of the Company in London to participate in the celebration.[21] It was a memorable occasion, the last time that any American group can do it, since the following day the Governor announced that the headquarters and archives of the Company were moving to Winnipeg.[22] The close of an era marked the beginning of a new one. Now, for the student of fur-trade history, or for one who would check the records for a project such as this — the place of the Scot in northwest history — Winnipeg will be the mecca.

ARMORIAL BEARINGS
OF THE
Hudson's Bay Company.
INCORPORATED 2ʸᵈ MAY 1670.

Chapter Three

John McLoughlin: "White-headed Eagle"

MACKENZIE

The person who left the most indelible mark on the fur trade history of the Pacific Northwest was Dr. John McLoughlin, called by the Indians "the White-headed Eagle." McLoughlin was the Chief Factor at Fort Vancouver from 1824 to 1846, at a period when the post was the hub of a veritable empire, stretching south from Alaska to northern California and encompassing present-day Washington, Idaho, Montana and Oregon.[1]

He was born in Riviere du Loup, Quebec, the son of Angelique Fraser whose parents came from Scotland.[2] After his father's early death by drowning, both John and his brother David were trained in medicine with the help of their grandfather Fraser who sent them to be educated in Scotland. After John received his medical degree he returned to Canada where he became a partner in the North West Company. When the Northwest and Hudson's Bay Companies merged in 1824, McLoughlin was in charge of Fort William on Lake Superior. Named a chief factor for the HBC he was given supervision of the Columbia District, with headquarters on the Columbia River.

Working with the approval of Sir George Simpson, a fellow Scot who was governor of the HBC, he selected Fort Vancouver to become the central post. Controlling the enormous territory listed above, Fort Vancouver developed a large farm, orchards, gardens, dairies, a sawmill, a flouring mill, a shipyard, mechanics' shops, together with the people needed to handle all of these activities. All of this resulted in creating a surrounding village of some size. Ships from England arrived annually, bringing trade goods, and taking back to England the year's harvest of furs which had been gathered from the far-flung posts under Company control.

McLoughlin's fame rests not only upon his business acumen. He is honored for the generous and humane treatment he extended toward the missionaries and American settlers who arrived on the Oregon Trail. He also helped to maintain a steady peace among the Indian tribes. Credits were extended to all, friends or rivals, supplying the staples necessary to sustain life until crops could be harvested the following year. Single-handed, he *could* have delayed the American occupation of the Oregon country, and his superiors would have praised him. But he absolutely refused to withhold supplies from the starving emigrants who arrived at Vancouver, the end of the transcontinental trail.

How his hospitality impressed one missionary party was told by Narcissa Whitman, when she and her husband, Dr. Marcus Whitman, together with fellow missionaries Henry and Eliza Spalding, ended an exhausting overland journey at Fort Vancouver on September 12, 1836.[3] The Whitman party was greeted upon arrival by Dr. McLoughlin and by two other notable Scots who would leave strong marks on our regional history. They were James Douglas, McLoughlin's associate who would eventually become the first Governor of Vancouver Island, and Dr. William Fraser Tolmie, a young physician who had been sent by the Company to take over medical responsibilities from the overburdened McLoughlin. Tolmie would serve later as Factor at Fort Nisqually and Fort Victoria.

To the exhausted missionaries Fort Vancouver appeared as a shining oasis of plenty on the wilderness frontier. In her journal Narcissa Whitman said: "What a delightful place this is . . . what a contrast this to the rough barren sand plains through which we have so recently passed. Here we found fruit of every description — apples, peaches, grapes, pear, plum, and fig trees in abundance." Of the extensive gardens, she wrote: ". . . cucumbers, melons, beans, peas, beets, cabbages, tomatoes, and every kind of vegetable too numerous to be mentioned." A tour of the fields and barns was impressive: "They estimate their wheat crop at 4,000 bushels this year, peas, the same. Oats and barley between 15 & 1,700 bushels each. The potato and turnip fields are large and fine. Their cattle are numerous, estimated at 1,000 head in all their settlements, also sheep & goats, but the sheep are of an inferior kind. We find also hens, turkeys, pigeons, but no geese."[4] She may not have known it since she didn't mention them, but the Company at that time also had three hundred hogs.

Narcissa went on to describe the dairy, the gristmill, and the storehouse filled with merchandise, exulting in the great variety from which she and her husband could select the necessities for establishing a new mission up the Columbia, at a place named Waiilatpu, the "Place of the Rye Grass." To all of this feast of the eyes, McLoughlin added his famed hospitality, entertaining the Whitman party at sumptuous meals at his own table, together with James Douglas, Dr. Tolmie, and their wives. To the weary travelers, forerunners of the American invasion of the Oregon country, McLoughlin gave unstinted help, as he would do later for successive waves of emigrants.

His generosity often went unpaid, costing the Company many losses. After the settlement of the Oregon boundary by treaty in 1846 he left the Company service, retiring under severe criticism. (Another chapter contains a letter written by one of his former colleagues years afterward which still bore signs of the bitterness felt by those he left behind.)

McLoughlin filed a land claim with the Oregon Provisional Government at the falls of the Willamette. Here he built a sawmill and laid out a townsite which would become Oregon City. He also announced his intention to become an American citizen, but the land claim was contested, and in 1850, following passage by Congress of the Donation Land Act, his claim was invalidated.[5] He was not forced to move and, in fact, Mc-Loughlin House is an historic treasure still, open to the public as a museum. He died in 1857, unrequited and embittered. Five years after his death his heirs finally received title to his property.

The gratitude of the Americans eluded him in life, but his towering figure stands today in Statuary Hall in the national Capitol, belated recognition of Oregon's great debt to one who, as much as any other individual, contributed to the opening of the Oregon country.[6] The "White-headed Eagle" is secure in history, for, as W. Kaye Lamb put it, "His career spanned a continent and embraced an entire period in the history of the Pacific Northwest."[7]

John McLoughlin from the James A. Wenn collection — Washington State Historical Society

Chapter Four

Transition

CAMPBELL

Adaptation to life in the new land was not easy. Perhaps nowhere were the problems underscored so dramatically as in the years surrounding the settlement of the claims of the Hudson's Bay Company and its affiliate, the Puget Sound Agricultural Company. Some HBC men chose to remain with the Company, such as Dr. William Fraser Tolmie;[1] others opted for American citizenship. Letters to, from or about them provide evidence of the difficulties of assimilation into the new *American* phase, or, by contrast, the last-ditch struggles of some to resist being swallowed by aggressive American expansionism.

In the Thomas Chambers collection in the Washington State Historical Society there are three letters from Tolmie, written in 1849 from Fort Nisqually where Tolmie was serving as Chief Factor for the Hudson's Bay Company post.[2] The first two are friendly, chatty, and informative, dealing not only with local affairs but also passing along to the American settler news of events in Europe.

The second letter bears Tolmie's solicitations concerning the theft and death of Chambers' prize horse, together with an offer "to assist you in discovering the skulking rascal who has committed the deed." He mentions that Judge Thornton, sub-agent for Indian affairs for the country north of the Columbia, had just arrived at Fort Nisqually, for the purpose of visiting "the Sound Indians as well as those of this neighborhood." The Judge suggested that Chambers "ride across to see him," with the understanding that he will help Chambers to get to the bottom of the affair. Tolmie closes with "kind regards to Mrs. C." (Chambers).

Four months elapse, and the next letter offers a startling change in tone and content. One must remember that the bill to organize Oregon territory had been passed by the Congress and signed into law by President Polk just one year before. The fate of Hudson's Bay Company holdings would not be settled for some time, though the treaty between Great Britain and the United States, signed in 1846, confirmed both the Hudson's Bay Company and the Puget Sound Agricultural Company in their holdings. Now, in 1849, HBC headquarters had been moved from Fort Vancouver, on the Columbia, to Victoria. Fort Nisqually was left, a British island in the sea of American expansion. Nearby, on lands once owned by the Puget Sound Agricultural Company, Fort Steilacoom had been built to house American troops. Tolmie was under enormous pressure, trying to hold Company property intact in the face of almost daily encroachments. Here is the last letter to Thomas Chambers.

Fort Nisqually Dec. 20th, 1849

Sir

   I hereby warn you, that in taking possession of or improving the claim of land you have lately been at work upon at Steilacoom Pugets Sound you are trespassing on the lands secured to the Pugets' Sound Company by the late Boundary Treaty betwixt Great Britain and the United States of America, which confirms to the Pugets' Sound Company their farms, lands, and other property of every description — The house you have roofed at Steilacoom as well as the ploughed land adjoining it are parts of an improvement, made by the said Company at Steilacoom several years prior to the settlement of the N.W. Boundary question between our respective countries.

I remain Sir
Respectfully Yours
(signed)
Wm. F. Tolmie

   Here, in miniature, is the problem — one stubborn Scot, clinging to principles of duty and loyalty to the old order and refusing to surrender to the new, as represented by the acceleration of American settlement on Puget Sound. He held out for nearly ten more years, but finally moved to Victoria in 1859 where he took charge of Company farms on Vancouver Island. For his faithful services he was appointed as one of the three members of the Board of Management of the Hudson's Bay Company. He retired in 1870, after nearly four decades of association with the Company, which in 1870, was 200 years old.[3]

   On the other side of the story was Dr. John McLoughlin, the powerful Chief Factor for many years at Fort Vancouver, which, during his tenure, was the hub of a veritable fur-trade empire. He, like Tolmie, received his medical education in Scotland prior to entering the fur trade. McLoughlin's generous treatment of the missionaries and settlers who came west on the Oregon Trail has been cited, as well as his famous hospitality at Fort Vancouver. Since his loans of seed, staples, and stock to the Americans often went unpaid, his generosity cost the Company many losses. *That* might have been forgiven. But, when he chose to leave the Company service after the settlement of the Oregon Boundary question, and filed a land claim with the Oregon provisional government, he came under severe criticism from his former colleagues. Years later, in writing to Dr. Tolmie, Archibald McKinlay, who had been in service at Fort Walla Walla until 1846, had this to say (the extract is from a letter written from Lake La Hache, British Columbia where McKinlay had settled after retirement from the HBC). It is dated 1884, nearly 40 years after

McLoughlin left the Company, but the bitterness remains in one of those he left behind.

". . . Now for the questions about the Hyas Doctor. Undoubtedly the Directors must have found much fault with the Doctor for the very reckless manner in which he made advances but I feel more than certain that the Oregon City claim by the Doctor and the building of the Mills was the main cause of the break between him and them. His rough treatment of the immigrants sent from B.C. to settle north of the Columbia also gave much offence and *entre nous* the Doctor did not show such a spirit of philanthropy in his dealings as he gets credit for. He did not search out the poor and needy; he made advances to everyone who asked without taking their need into consideration . . . I cannot say that the old Gent was timid but one trait in his character was painfully observable — his obsequence to his enemies and neglect of his friends. I do not remember one instance of his showing any Philanthropic tendency after his retirement from the H.B.C. and from the way in which he fed his faithful servants on food scarsely (sic) fit for hogs while of thousands of cattle and ten thousands of flour they never tasted . . . in my humble opinion Douglas could have managed affairs just as well without any such lavish advances. Those advances were discontinued when the Doc retired, still things moved along as smoothly as before. The Doc did gossip much about his grievances to Americans. He always held out as much as that."[4]

The reference to "Douglas" was to James Douglas, McLoughlin's successor at Fort Vancouver, later to be the first Governor of Vancouver Island. From the vantage of time, it is difficult, though not impossible, to analyze the conflicting opinions of McLoughlin's character as given by Archibald McKinlay, or by the Oregonians who nominated "the White-Headed Eagle" to represent their state in Statuary Hall, in the Capitol rotunda in Washington, D.C.

McKinlay had a reason for his unkind blast at McLoughlin, having experienced the Doctor's whiplash after trying to drive a sharp bargain with some American emigrants while he was in charge in 1843 at Fort Walla Walla. William Sampson recounts the episode in *John McLoughlin's Business Correspondence, 1847-1848.*[5] McLoughlin manfully accepted responsibility for his statement to Peter Burnett, an Oregon emigrant of 1843, in which he said that, in the matter of a cattle bargain, "Mr. Mc-Kindlay (sic) did wrong and I will not consent to profit by your Reliance on our Good faith." Burnett's account appeared in his published journal, a part of *An Account and History of the Oregon Territory*, written by George Wilkes, in 1846. McKinlay had written McLoughlin demanding an explanation, and the doughty Doctor had replied, though certainly not to

26

McKinlay's satisfaction. The letter came from Oregon City in 1847, meaning that the story had appeared, been digested by McKinlay, who asked for clarification from McLoughlin, and received his reply within a year from publication — not bad timing for the Oregon frontier of 1847!

McLoughlin's other correspondence from Oregon City frequently contains references to "Land Claim Jumpers" who harrassed him and other recorded settlers. In a letter to his friend Nathaniel Wyeth he referred to the way he had aided American missionaries when they first came to the Oregon country. Now, in 1847, he said that the Methodist Mission was doing its best to carve up his land grant[6] A man named A. J. Vickers had settled on 274 acres which had been farmed, in part, by McLoughlin. Despite local efforts to deal with such "Jumpers," the matter wound up in a lawsuit. Then, in 1850, upon passage of the Donation Land Act, McLoughlin's claim was invalidated. He was not forced to move but it was five years after his death in 1857 before his heirs finally received title to his property. McLoughlin's bitter experience was repeated by others who had left the Hudson's Bay Company. Though many sought and acquired American citizenship, the American settlers' lingering resentments over one-time Hudson's Bay Company monopoly in the Oregon country perpetuated a competitive and vengeful reaction in dealings with the former HBC men.

The letters of Edward Huggins, last Factor at Fort Nisqually who became an American citizen, was elected Auditor of Pierce County, and who served as county commissioner for three terms, are an eloquent witness. Huggins was English by birth, not a Scot, but his HBC background, particularly after he succeeded Dr. Tolmie at Nisqually, led to the usual irritations. These tended to surface most regularly during political campaigns, naturally enough, when some benighted *locofoco* could call slighting attention to Huggins' imperial past. But Huggins was a calmer soul than Dr. McLoughlin had been, contenting himself with writing occasional articles about local history for the *Tacoma Ledger*. He always took pleasure in correcting the mythology which was being perpetuated by some of the early settlers, a notable example being the stories which grew up around the trial and execution of Leschi, chief of the Nisqually Indians. Huggins was convinced that Leschi had been sacrificed to appease the citizenry after the Indian war of 1855. Modern historians tend to agree with Huggins' judgment of the affair.

In another *Tacoma Ledger* story, written by a friend of Leschi, Edward Huggins, and Dr. Tolmie (all in the person of the redoubtable pioneer, Ezra Meeker) is a rather poignant account which symbolizes beautifully some of the elements at play in the lives of Leschi's Nisqually descendants, the now expatriate Dr. Tolmie, and Meeker, the prosperous American hop-grower.[8] In the biographical account of Tolmie, I mentioned that he had visited Meeker some forty years after his removal to Victoria. Meeker tells the story:

"Another incident of interest was developed upon the last visit of my old-time friend, Dr. W. F. Tolmie, at the time of which I have written (before), the Hudson's Bay Company's factor at Nisqually but later of Victoria, B.C. The Doctor came to Puyallup and stayed several days while collecting data for a historical work on the Indians. (Tolmie mentioned just *one* day as Meeker's guest: Ed. note) It was during the hop picking time, and I had 180 Indians at work in one field. We went out to the field the first day and were soon surrounded with the whole band, some crying for joy, some laughing, and all greatly excited at the sight of their long-lost friend, whom they had not seen for more than twenty years. (Ed. note: Tolmie's journal said that he had not been back for nearly 40 years.) The doctor could speak their language as fluently as any of them. It was remarkable, the intimate knowledge of the different individuals retained by him. The conference lasted a long time and was carried on in the Indian tongue, and I never knew what transpired except as told me by the doctor. After we had returned to the house he said, 'Do you know that you have all the descendants of Leschi here with you?' I told him I did not. He believed that in some way, they, the younger ones had acquired an intimate knowledge as to the friend of their great ancestor, though they said they had not thought about it."

The Indians knew that Ezra Meeker had sat on the jury in the first trial of Leschi, and that he had voted to acquit him of the charges. The trial ended in a hung jury and the jury was dismissed. Though the first trial was held in Steilacoom, the second was moved to Olympia, with a new jury sitting — one which did not include Meeker or the other juror who had voted for acquittal. This time Leschi was convicted and executed, fifteen months after he had been remanded to military custody. Meeker referred to the event as "atrocious judicial murder." He continued for the rest of his life to proclaim Leschi's innocence, years later writing a book whose subtitle was "The Tragedy of Leschi."[9] Though Tolmie's visit predated this publication by many years, Leschi's family and friends never forgot either Meeker's or Tolmie's stand in the controversial episode.

Tolmie's welcome by the hop-picking Indians reflected another important truth: a long history of fair dealing by the Hudson's Bay Company with the Indians of Puget Sound. The old Scotsman could return to Victoria warmed by the recognition he had received from the Indian friends he had not seen for many years.

Chapter Five

Scottish folk customs

GORDON

The richness of American life depends upon the mingling of cultures from many countries. The old "melting pot" theory, in which these cultures were supposed to fade away until one homogenized America emerged, is no longer valid, if it ever was.

Richard Dorson has spoken about "the mingling of folklore repertoires that flourishes along national borders, a phenomenon rarely observed by folklorists in the field. In northern New England and the Great Lakes states, French Canadian folk culture, nourished from the Province of Quebec, has spilled over into the United States."[1]

The same process can be observed in the Hispanic traditions that flourish on the borders between the American southwest and Mexico. The phenomenon can also be found on the borders of the Pacific Northwest and the three western Canadian provinces, which are strong in Scottish settlement and tradition. In British Columbia, for example, there are 79 place-names derived from Scottish surnames, plus 30 place-names after actual places in Scotland. Saskatchewan has 102 based on Scottish surnames, and 42 place-names after places in Scotland. Alberta has 71 names based on surnames, plus 31 named for Scottish places. Only Ontario, in eastern Canada, shows more Scottish influence in terms of place-names than the three western Canadian provinces.[2]

In the Pacific Northwest geographical names are instant clues to the patterns of early settlement. We begin with an abundance of Indian names. Then came the Spanish explorers, and, though many Spanish place-names are now obsolete, some do remain, such as the Strait of Juan de Fuca and Rosario. The British explorers, particularly Captain George Vancouver, gave many names to the Puget Sound region: Mt. Rainier, Vashon, Port Townsend, to name a few. The American explorers, such as Lieutenant Charles Wilkes and the United States Exploring Expedition, added more, such as Commencement Bay, near Tacoma.[3]

Most of the Scottish names in the Pacific Northwest were based upon Scottish surnames or actual places in Scotland. One American president of Scottish heritage was honored by the county named after him: U. S. Grant. The towns of Aberdeen, McCleary, McKenna, McMurray, Fife and Roy are remnants of the Scottish passage. Douglas County, Granger, Wilkeson and Winthrop are probable Scottish derivatives. We also have Tolmie Peak, a foothill of Mt. Rainier, named for the Hudson's Bay Company factor at Fort Nisqually.[4] There is another Mount Tolmie within the city limits of Victoria in British Columbia. Oregon has a number of Scottish place-names, some named for early fur-traders, others for pioneer settlers.[5] In general, however, there are not too many names of Scottish origin in the northwestern states, at least as compared to the western

Canadian provinces.

How many characteristics, customs, folklore, including songs and legends, are still peculiar to the Scot transplanted to the northwest? What Scottish flavor remains? This is far from a new question — the retention or disappearance of ethnic differences. As early as the beginning of the nineteenth century, writers in Scotland were concerned. One of them, Henry Cockburn, said: "He saw many things that were purely Scottish in the capital society, that is, speaking of Edinburgh, passing away; manners and fashions becoming increasingly assimilated to those of polite society throughout the United Kingdom. He believed, too, that it was largely inevitable. But he also regretted that Scottish national characteristics could be thrown into this rough melting pot after so many centuries of proud differentiation. He spoke for many when he wrote in his journal: 'The prolongation of Scottish peculiarities, especially of our language and habits, I do earnestly desire. An exact knowledge and feeling of what those have been since 1707 until now would be more curious 500 years hence than a similar knowledge and feeling of the old Greeks. But the features and expression of a people cannot be perpetuated by legislative engraving. Nothing can prevent the gradual disappearance of local manners under the absorption and assimilation of a far larger, richer and more powerful adjoining kingdom. Burns and Scott have done more for the preservation of historic Scotland than could ever be accomplished by law, statesmen or associations."[6]

Cockburn did not give much credit to social organizations when it came to preserving Scottish customs. But no one could prevent the transplanted Scot from trying. The various societies which were formed, such as the Caledonian Society, the St. Andrews Society, the Bonnie Doones, attempted to perpetuate Scottish tradition. There were also other, less formal societies. Such a one, and fairly typical, was the Cronies Club, organized in Tacoma in the 1880's.

The members were all early settlers of Tacoma, if late 19th century can be considered "early." In a rare little history of the Club, brought to my attention by a grandson of Frank Cameron, who was a Club founder, the "Introduction" states that "the Club grew out of long and intimate association of a number of Scots in Tacoma perpetuating the glories of Scotland year after year by commemorations of Robert Burns' birthday and of St. Andrews' Day. These zealous and patriotic efforts developed into the Caledonian and St. Andrews Societies."[7]

Their guilding theme was expressed in a song by Thomas D'Arcy McGee, a Canadian statesman. It was called *Salutation to the Celts*. The mingled pride and sadness of the Scot in exile is there:

Hail to our Celtic brethren, wherever they may be,
In the far woods of Oregon or o'er the Atlantic sea;
Whether they guard the banners of St. George in Indian vales,
Or spread beneath the nightless North experimental sails—
 One in name and in fame
 Are the sea-divided Gaels.

In the tradition of the immortal Robert Burns the members of the Club regaled each other with songs and stories, some of which they composed themselves. The song, *Cronies O' Mine,* contained a salute to a single member of the Club in every stanza. The song was written, of course, in Scots dialect: "There's Geordie Dickson, oor auld pioneer, wha came tae Tacoma, '82 was the year," or following, "the finest braw fellow under the sun, tae meet wi', and crack wi', an' hae some fun."

A tribute to Frank Cameron reads: "to the Chief o' Lochiel," and "wha's heart is as true as the Cameron steel; a fine auld chap, an' the best O' men, an' we'll a' sing 'The March o' the Cameron Men.'"[8]

"When Drummond dons his Tartan" is a lengthy tribute to Alexander Drummond, organizer of the Club, "Keeper of the Flame of Scottish Pride:" "While in between the songs we love are sung, the songs that mak' us feel we still are young; bright quip an' jest an' weel-told humorous story serve to round oot oor evenin's repertory; as Burns would say, we're feelin' glorious, owre a' the ills o' life victorious, when Drummond dons his Tartan."

No credit to editor or compiler is given in the little book.[9] But, considering the fact that there are *two* pictures of Sandy Drummond and only one of every other member . . . your guess is as good as mine. The "Cronies" were a successful group with ties to most of Tacoma civic life. Perhaps they were fairly typical of the transplanted Scot who found security and success in the Pacific Northwest. In fact, so secure were they that they even admitted two Irish "Cronies" into the Club as "Honorary Scotsmen." One was John Arthur, attorney and past president of the Washing State Bar Association; the other was James Murphy, leading dry-goods merchant. The other members were James Neil, a printer originally from Glasgow; Phipps Keith, machine tool manufacturer; David Healy, a tea importer from Ayrshire; Tom Hurley, from Glasgow, in the plumbing business; Henry Coubrough, of the Northwestern Dock Company, from Stirling; Francis Cameron, from Strathspey, an industrial broker; David Macarthur, executive of the Great Northern Railway, from Glasgow; Robert Montgomery, publisher of the *Puyallup Valley Tribune,* and a prolific author; George Dickson and Alexander Drummond, both owners of prosperous clothing stores; George MacMartin, real estate broker; and Robert MacQuarrie, lumber mill owner.

One thing they all had in common — ambition and enterprise, plus a certain "Horatio Alger" quality which may have spurred them all to emigrate to the far northwest to seek fortune or fame. On Puget Sound and Commencement Bay, they became a part of the Establishment.[10] I'd like to have known them.

THRIFT

Peebles Body (to Townsman who was supposed to be in London on a visit): ' E-eh, Mac! Ye're sune hame again! '

Mac.: ' E-eh, it's just a ruinous place, that! Mun, a had na' been the-erre abune Twa Hoours when— BANG—went SAXPENCE! '

A Victorian version of perhaps the oldest ' Scotch ' joke of them all. Drawn by Charles Keene (1823-1891)

1—Alexander MacKenzie; 2—Washington Irving; 3—William Fraser Tolmie; 4—Frances Simpson; 5—George Abernethy; 6—David Douglas; 7—Susan Allison; 8—Archibald Menzies; 9—Sir James Douglas; 10—John Muir; 11—Earl of Selkirk; 12—James Cook; 13—John Paul Jones.

Chapter Six

Traditional observances

FRAZER

The birthday of Robert Burns is a great occasion on which Scots love to gather in honor of the national poet. Old friendships are renewed and new acquaintances made. Much goes into the preparation of a traditional Scottish menu and "the glass goes round" in toasts. Here are a few of the toasts one may hear that festive night: "Here's health, wealth, wit, an' meal;" or "Here's the Land O' the Bens, the Glens, an' the Heroes!" Another favorite is "Here's ta them that loves, or lends us a lift!" A more poetic glass-raiser is "Here's ta the heath, the hill, an' the heather, the bonnet, the plaidie, the kilt, an' the feather! Here's to the Song that Auld Scotland can boast, may her name never die — that's a Highlandman's boast."

And a short, pithy one: "Blithe may we a' be, ill may we never see!" There are dozens of other toasts but this gives one an idea.[1]

A typical menu served at a recent Burns Night included such delicacies as "braised steak Caledonian" and "Scotch trifle" but the course of honor was the haggis. A haggis is the lining of a sheep's belly, filled with a kind of suet pudding, and all good Scots are supposed to be enamored of this dish. There is a poem called "The Haggis is a wondrous Beast" and it has something to do with the Haggis falling in love with a suet pudding! Its lines are so improbable that I will refrain from quoting them.[2]

The entertainment at a "Burns Night" generally consists of songs and ballads of the Bard rendered by people who are considered not only good singers or recitalists but who possess an authentic accent. Before the dinner begins it is customary to say "the Selkirk Grace," of ancient tradition. It reads "Some hae meat and cannot eat, and some wad eat that want it; but we hae meat and we can eat, and say the Lord be thankit." More words were added by a Mr. R. R. Walker, of Scone, Scotland, who has always admired the Selkirk Grace but thought it did not go far enough: "Some hae meat and cannot eat, and some wad eat that want it; but we hae meat and we can eat, yet take it a' for granted. So Lord, we pray, as come it may, as come it will for a' that, that we can spare an ample share for a' that want, and a' that."[3] Another custom is "Addressing the Haggis," complete with piper, parade, and the first cut with a ceremonial dirk.

St. Andrew's Day is a festival of the national saint of Scotland. Since the Reformation the holiday has become more of a politicai than a religious celebration. For several hundred years Scots "went St. Andrewing" on November 30th, setting off in the morning to hunt rabbits and squirrels, returning to end a convivial day with feasting and drinking. The day is celebrated in the Pacific Northwest in a most interdenominational way. People who attend are not necessarily Presbyterians or members of the

Church of Scotland. (The last time the event was held here it was hosted by the Unitarian Church.) Another event is the "Betwixt and Between Party," generally held a couple of days after Christmas.[4]

The Highland Games have been imported bodily from Scotland and are held throughout Canada and the United States.[5] Pipers, dancers, athletes and spectators get ready every year for the traditional games held in Seattle. They are sponsored by various Scottish groups, such as the Caledonian Society, the Highlanders, the Daughters of Scotia, and the Bonnie Doones. Athletes compete in certain events, such as the hammer throw, and the "caber toss." The games are always followed by dancing and piping, with pipe bands coming great distances to take part.

Another great ethnic event is "the Gathering of the Clans." Individual clans have their own reunions, sometimes scheduled back in Scotland, and clan members come from all over the world to participate. In 1975, for example, the McClennan Clan met in "Clan Parliament" for the first gathering in three hundred and thirty years. The McClennans, who scattered after the defeat of 1645 in the battle between England and Scotland, came from Australia, South Africa, Japan, Canada, and the United States, to meet in Inverness. Eighteen hundred people attended, including members from the Pacific Northwest. All were impressed by the magnificence of the spectacle. At the clan parliament meeting plans were laid to regain some ancestral lands in Kintail by purchase from the National Trust of Scotland. Church services were held, partly in Gaelic, followed by a formal dinner and dance. Clan members visited the sites of the battles of Culloden and Aldern, where many of the family fought for Lord Seaforth.[6]

The origins of the Scottish tartan is always of interest to those concerned about Scottish customs. Individual sets or patterns were first associated with the districts where they were made, and only later became identified with the name of the most prominent clan in the area. According to the *Guinness Book of Records*, the earliest evidence of tartan was the so-called Feldkirk Tartan which first appeared about 245 A.D. It was a piece in a light and dark brown pattern which was found stuffed in a jar of coins in Belle's Meadow, north of Calendar Park in Scotland. The first written reference to Highland dress occurred in a saga from 1093 A.D. The word "Tartan" comes from the French word "tartain," a name for a certain kind of material, regardless of color or pattern. Later the word became more specialized when Highland tartan acquired distinctive checkered patterns. The Gaelic word for tartan was "breacan," meaning partly colored or speckled. In any case, the bright designs have become associated historically with the different clans, bearing all manner of patriotic associations for those entitled to wear them.[7] This is as true in the Pacific

Northwest as anywhere else, and the special occasions, such as the Highland Games, Burns Night, St. Andrew's Day, and "the gatherings" are always graced by the colorful tartan. Pipe bands lead the way, with the Black Watch, the Seaforth Highlanders, the Clan Gordon Band, the Keith Pipe Band being among those present at Scottish events in Seattle and Tacoma.

When Scots in Hawaii joined their fellow citizens in 1976 to celebrate the Chinese New Year, or the "Year of the Dragon," the Caledonian Society had a special party to celebrate the mystery of Scotland's own favorite creature, the "Loch Ness Monster."[8] Scots from Washington State caught the message and joined in, celebrating the dragon and the mythical sea serpent simultaneously — a fine ethnic mix, if there ever was one!

A Wee Bit O' Scotland
at the
15th Annual
Tartan Ball
of the
Clan Gordon Pipe Band

SATURDAY 25 FEBRUARY
AT THE
TACOMA BICENTENNIAL PAVILION
8:30 PM — 1:00 AM

Featuring the Pipes, Drums and Dancers
of
- TACOMA'S CLAN GORDON PIPE BAND
- SEATTLE PIPE BAND
- PORTLAND'S CLAN MacLEAY
- OLYMPIA HIGHLANDERS
- BREMERTON GRENADIERS

Dance to the Music of Reg Hudman and His Orchestra In the Glenn Miller Style

Chapter Seven

Scottish proverbs

MACPHERSON

"Who teaches himself has a fool for a master" may be a debatable statement to a self-made man but is certainly in the tradition of Scottish proverbs. Some proverbs have passed on into everyday usage in plain English, being so familiar as to make us forget that their beginnings were proverbial. Such a proverb is the saying "a tumbling stone never gathers fog." The word "fog" is Gaelic for "moss," so today we hear "a rolling stone gathers no moss." Another is "all comparisons are odious," meaning that comparisons can hardly be made without disparagement to one of the parties being compared.

The "wisdom" quoted above was taken from a book of Scottish proverbs which was printed in 1718[1] Published at a time when a number of four-letter words were in common usage, the collection poses problems for the author who would use them in a modern book. Having no desire to be accused of corrupting young minds I will select just a few printable proverbs, ignoring those that verge on the obscene. By that I do not mean that those used here were altered or expurgated, only that they are selective. Anyone who feels cheated can find his *own* book of proverbs.

My grandmother, Susie Murdock, used to tell how *her* grandmother used to stop by on her way home from shopping. She lived on a hill overlooking Hornell in western New York state. Her greeting invariably would be "Susie, will ye gie me a coop o' tae to help me up the hill?" Not long ago I learned that this was really a paraphrase of a proverb which goes something like "good legs and strong tea will master many a hill." Mountain climbers of Rainier and Baker will attest to the truth of that.

James Kelly, the author of the old book of proverbs said "there are current in society upwards of 3,000 proverbs, exclusively Scottish . . . the Scots are wonderfully given to this way of speaking, and as the consequence of that, abound with proverbs, many of which are very expressive, quick, and home to the purpose; and, indeed, this humour prevails universally over the entire nation." He goes on to say ". . . to that manner of speaking I was used from my infancy, and that to such a degree, that I became, in some measure, remarkable for it."[2]

Proverbs, like folk songs, travel. The author said, "sometimes what I believed to be Scottish proverbs were not only English but French, Italian, Spanish, Latin and Greek proverbs; for the sense and sentiments of mankind, as to the main concerns of life, are much the same, and their observations about them, being often repeated, become proverbs, which, though differing in words, express the same thoughts . . . therefore I found myself obliged to set down all those for Scottish proverbs that are *used* in Scotland."

He then goes on to say, "I have left out all those which are openly obscene, and these are very many, pat, and expressive. But since it does not become a man of manners to use them, it does not become a man of my age and profession to write them." Judging from the shockers he included one wonders what one had to say to be censored! He also gave the rules which governed his choices: no blasphemy, none to cause "supertitious dread," though there are many about the devil, witchcraft, and spells, or those sayings which were "silly and useless," such as "go fiddle my dog a dance." He also wanted the meaning clear for those he rendered, so "wrote the English words in the margins that correspond to the Scottish words in the proverbs;" changed such as "stane" to "stone," "bean" to "bone," "mair" to "more," etc.[3]

Discussing the proverbs listed here with northwestern Scots produced many a knowing chuckle, and a few more. Second generation Scots recalled their fathers or mothers or relatives using them, or others like them. Quite a list could be compiled of those still in use among Scots of the northwest, especially among people who came here from the southeastern mountains of the United States. Those sayings may have undergone a double "sea-change." Here are a few, for flavor, if not for the main course which awaits you if you look for more.

"All your geese are swans." The author explains, "to those highly conceited of what is their own."

"A penny-weight of love is worth a pound-weight of law." The author says, "against lawsuits."

"A winter's night, a woman's mind, and a laird's purpose change oft."

"A Scotch mist will wet an Englishman to the skin."

"A dog's life, mickle hunger, mickle ease." Or, as we might say, "He's lazy — no work, no eat."

"Danger past and God forgotten." A good example of "foxhole religion," when the soldier under fire finds it easy to pray.

"You never saw green cheese but your teeth watered." The author said, "to those who covet something from us."

"You'd have hit it if you had a stick," meaning, of course, "to hit the nail on the head."

"You tied a knot with your tongue you cannot loose with your teeth," (comment to newly-weds).

"Your wind shakes no corn." Spoken to a boaster, and the Scot calls boasters or braggarts "windy people."

"You look like the devil in daylight." Meaning Beelzebub, or Old Scratch, or take your pick, he has a thousand names.

"You are an honest man, and I'm your brother, and that's two lies."

"You come a day after the fair." The author said, "after the proper season is over."

"If you canna bite dinna show your teeth."

"A lazy cat makes a proud mouse."[4]

That should be enough to whet an appetite for more. Any student of ethnic history could have much fun and perhaps preserve a dying tradition by collecting the proverbial sayings of his own ethnic group. One could search his own mind, question a member of an earlier generation of the family, or a friend of the same heritage, to begin a fascinating collection. Proverbs are clues to history, folklore and national character.[5]

Chapter Eight

Things that go "Bump"

Ghosts, goblins, "wraiths and kelpies" were all too familiar to the Scot by the misty glens of the Highlands or the legend-shrouded streams of the Lowlands. Sometimes, when the Scot uprooted and moved to the Pacific Northwest, the ghostly company followed right along, kept alive in song and story. More than one beloved ballad has a ghost or super-natural being in it. The superstitions which are a part of the Celtic herit-age die hard.

Did you ever wonder about not walking under a ladder? In folklore the Scot believed that ladders are associated with images of violent death. Not that one may fall on you — that would be too easy. At one time, dark ages ago, the fear of walking too close or under a ladder was the fear of ending one's life on the gallows. In the earliest days people were hanged for the most minor offences. A person who walks under a ladder is walking literally "in the shadow of death." Ladders were also used dur-ing the witchcraft mania in executions by burning. A witch was tied to a ladder which either stood over the pyre, or was lowered into it.[1]

The witchcraft mania finally waned but the superstitions lingered on. A century after the mania passed, Robert Burns wrote a poem telling how the devil could be summoned.[2] Then Sir Walter Scott wrote a book called *Letters on Demonology and Witchcraft*.[3] Both were published dur-ing the Scottish "Enlightenment," by which time reason had supposedly banished superstition. These artistic efforts were built on irony, but many of the readers missed the irony, finding instead a confirmation of the old dark beliefs.

One can tour the British Isles today, Scotland in particular, and see pointed out the various sites where famous "Covens" of witches and war-locks used to meet; examples of "devils" cauldrons, where rushing streams boil without apparent reason; vaults and burial places where the victims or the condemned were interred; gloomy crypts of famous cathedrals, fill-ed with spooky effigies of the departed, where guides love to point out grisly legends from the dark days, generally in dark, sepulchural voices. There are many spine-tickling, vestigial remains of the ancient supernatur-al folklore — pun intended.

Recently the British Travel Service published a guide to the haunted castles or houses of the British Isles. There were more than five hundred listed.[4] Many of them were in Scotland. There are, of course, more haunt-ed places than *that* — these are the ones that have been verified!

The Evil Eye

More than the Scots have the tradition of the "Evil Eye." The super-stition is known throughout Europe. It is said to be "the possession of certain persons of envious disposition, whose glance holds a withering and injurious quality which, when directed upon the goods, cattle, or children of more fortunate people, cause them to decay, or affect them with mysterious ailments so that they fall into decline or even perish." As recently as the early twentieth century, the superstition was reported in the small township of Duthill in Inverness where "plenty of people round about us have got the Evil Eye and hurt both cattle and people with it." One student of Scottish folklore learned in oral interviews that it "still exists in Caithness, Sutherland, Ross-shire, Lewis, Harris, both Uists, Skye, Tiree, and Islay."[5]

Scots who moved here are said to use the "Evil Eye" for political purposes only, but that practice, I might add, is hardly restricted to Scots. The practice was absorbed by tactics of vituperation against one's political enemies, such as the famous case of Senator James Nesmith, of Oregon. Of Scottish descent, the Senator once issued a challenge to a political opponent in rhetoric unmatched by any of the Harpies who called down the wrath of the gods on hapless aspirants to office: "TO THE WORLD!!! J. QUINN THORNTON, having resorted to low, cowardly and dishonorable means, for the purpose of injuring my character and standing, and having refused honorable satisfaction, which I have demanded: I avail myself of this opportunity of publishing him to the world as a reclaimless liar, an infamous scoundrel, a black hearted villain, an arrant coward, a worthless vagabond and an imported miscreant, a disgrace to the profession and a dishonor to his country. JAMES W. NESMITH, Oregon City, June 7, 1847."[6]

With literary talent like that, who needed an "Evil Eye?"

It was thought that women were most often the owners of the "ill e'e," as it was often called, rather than men. The Evil Eye was generally considered to be a hereditary possession, descending from father to daughter, or from mother to son. The belief also persisted that some kind of magical knowledge, or secret spell concerning its use and function, was handed down from one generation to another. There were many stories of experiences, mostly tragic, of being injured by the Evil Eye, or knowing someone who had been. Up to now, I have been unable to find any Scottish emigrant, or descendant of one, who will admit to a belief in the Evil Eye, though one suggested that since the power was hereditary, if they had it in Scotland, they must have it here! Two other informants suggested that such powers *may* have existed in Scotland but they saw no evidence of their existence in America.

Folk Medicine

There are thousands of cures. Some have to do with healing sick sheep or cattle. "Curing the murrain," a distemper in cattle, sometimes called "the hasty," since the cattle died very soon after being attacked by it, could be accomplished by "a need-fire." Elaborate instructions for creating the fire, whose smoke had power to free the suffering cattle from "the murrain," were followed. It has been suggested that this practice may be a hangover from the raising of the sacred fire of the Druids annually on May Day.[7]

Hydrophobia caused by the bite of a mad dog had its own powerful cure. The recipe called for the use of two quarts of ale or wine, red sage or rue, twelve cloves of garlic, and London treacle — all easily available from your corner grocery store. Boiled, corked in bottles and kept a year, the dose is three spoonfuls morning and night until a pint is used up. This should be sufficient for man or beast, according to the recipe. Another never-fail method is "Garlic, rue, and salt pounded together may be applied to the wound." Works every time.

Stopping a nosebleed calls for certain techniques. Some people were said to have the power to do it while miles away from the subject. Picking a certain leaf from a plant, opening the Bible and reading a verse from it, followed by breaking the leaf in two parts, were effective if one had the power to begin with. There is a story in my own family about Uncle Charlie who was present (I can't say *fought*) at the Battle of Gettysburg. When the battle began he developed a hard nosebleed. It bled for three days, off and on, sufficient to keep him behind the lines. Many miles away on a Pennsylvania farm, his mother and sisters, hearing the rumble of the cannon, prayed long and hard for Charlie, whose regiment they knew was there. They prayed for three days. Charlie's nosebleed stopped. But then, so had the cannon. Did anyone ever guess that the firing guns and the resulting concussion had anything to do with it? Being good Scots, probably not.

Second Sight

Once more, this peculiar talent is not limited to Scots. The power of "second sight" is given to people who "get glimpses into another world beyond the world of sense." They are persons of extraordinary sensitivity, called "fey" back in Scotland. The gift of prophecy goes with the power. The vision may come in any place, at any time of the day or night, and always without bidding. There are certain places in Scotland where all of the inhabitants are said to have the power, such as the island of Eriskay.

There were also famous seers whose prophecies are still being worked out, such as "the fall of the House of Seaforth," foretold by "Kenneth the Sallow" who lived during the 17th century. He predicted that in the last days of the Seaforth clan there would be "four great lairds . . . one shall be buck-toothed, another hare-lipped, another half-witted, and the fourth a stammerer . . . when he (the last chief) looks around and sees them, he may know that his sons are doomed to death, that his broad lands shall pass away to a stranger, and that his race shall come to an end." All that the seer predicted came to pass in time.[8]

As stated earlier, the Scot has no monopoly on second sight. A friend of mine from the bayou country of Louisiana foresees events from time to time and startles his fellow workers by prophecies which come true.[9] But, almost without exception, first generation Scots in the northwest believe in the power of second sight.

Superstitions that have to do with death are very common. One is surprised to see how some have been absorbed into general folklore, such as that the howling of a dog in the night heralds the approach of death; a bird tapping at a window is another sign of "death wanting into the house." The "laughter of an owl" means that someone in the neighborhood is going to die. Add the customs observed after a death, similar to the Irish wake, but not completely, where friends or family "sit up with corpse. They are given a Bible, a candle, food, and a bottle of whiskey. The clock is stopped, and any mirrors must be covered." Those who "sit up" must wait for dawn, and there must be no coming or going in the dark for fear of what might be seen.

"From ghoulies and ghosties and long-leggety beasties and things that go bump in the night, Good Lord, deliver us." The ancient Scottish prayer says it all![10]

The MacClurg Stone in Minnigaff Churchyard.

TO THE WORLD!!

J. Quinn Thornton,

Having resorted to low, cowardly and dishonorable means, for
the purpose of injuring my character and standing, and having
refused honorable satisfaction, which I have demanded; I avail
myself of this opportunity of publishing him to the world as a
reclaimless liar, an infamous scoundrel, a black hearted villain,
an arrant coward, a worthless vagabond and an imported miscreant, a disgrace to the profession and a dishonor to his country

JAMES W. NESMITH.

OREGON CITY, JUNE. 7. 1847

Chapter Nine

Ballads and folk songs: *a* potpourri

SCOTT

Orally transmitted over the centuries the traditional Scottish ballad came to America with the emigrating Scot. What Sir Walter Scott said about England could be applied to America in, "When the Blue Bonnets came Over the Border." William Dunbar said earlier: "Scotland had invaded England more than once, but the blue bonnets never went over the border so triumphantly as when they did so in the shape of songs and ballads."[1]

The ballads and folksongs brought to America from Scotland formed a rich depository of history and folklore. By its very nature a ballad tells a story. Many a Scottish ballad was based upon an actual historic episode, and, though many times the names and the facts got twisted in transmission from generation to generation, a great body of Scottish tradition was preserved and carried to America.[2] Most of the historical materials in Scottish balladry date from the 16th and 17th centuries. Thus many of the Scottish emigrants, from American colonial times onward, were bearers of the folk tradition as expressed by the ballad.

In Scotland the ballad flourished on the borders with England, in some instances celebrating victories over the English, in others the crushing defeats by the enemy to the south. (By use of such names as "Culloden," where the Scots took a pasting, a rallying cry was created i.e. the ballad as a political weapon.) Interestingly enough, our peaceful border with Canada also resulted in an exchange which includes a rich common heritage in folksong and balladry. The Canadians work a lot harder than we do to preserve ethnic traditions, weaving them into patterns of civic life. But through proximity and modern mobility, the strong Celtic heritage of western Canada is shared with Pacific Northwest friends south of the international boundary. There is much "criss-crossing" of the border, particularly for sharing in Scottish celebrations and traditional events like the Highland Games.

Not only do we have the "mingling of folklore repertoires that flourishes along national borders," as Richard Dorson was cited in a preceding chapter, we also had the westward movement. As America moved from its "Atlantic to its Pacific phase," as Bernard De Voto, historian of the westward movement observed, the migrating settlers brought ethnic traditions along. The mountains of the southeast, settled before the Revolution by Scottish emigrants, were rich depositories for the classic Scots ballad and folksong. Professor Francis Child traveled the whole region, collecting over one hundred ballads which have survived in oral tradition in America, nearly a third of the three hundred and five ballads he gathered and published.[3] The ballad was migrant, too, but then they always are, that being the nature of oral tradition. And when large numbers of these Scots moved west from Appalachia, pioneers on the trail brought the singing tradition with them.

Changes frequently occurred in the words and the musical line, as new geography and new customs supplanted the old. Such ballad classics as *Barbara Allen,* with interminable verses, *Lord Randal, Mary Hamilton* and others which once flourished along the Anglo-Scottish border can be heard today in Washington's Skagit, Okanagan, Stevenson and Cowlitz counties, places where Scots congregated.[4]

The folksong revival which swept America in the 1950's and continues unabated (though quieter), helped to revive interest in the ancient songs. The *repertoires* of such folksingers as Seattle's own Judy Collins, or Joan Baez, gave the songs new and glowing life. One example is *The Great Silkie,* a song from the Orkney Islands which perpetuates an Orkney myth about "the seal men" who came to shore, mated with humans, retreated again to the sea, only to die in a tragic resolution of the fate which befalls one who challenges the natural order.[5] No Orkneyman will eat seal meat, a taboo which the Hudson's Bay Company was forced to observe since many of their best employees were Orcadians.

Among the Scottish songs which flowered out of the northwestern experience several of the best are products of the fur-trade period, which is certainly unsurprising considering the part which Scots played in it. There was the beautiful *Boat Song,* sometimes known as *The Scot's Lament,* and sometimes attributed to John Galt, a Gallovidian who visited fur trade posts in the early 19th century.[6] It goes like this: "Listen to me as when ye heard your fathers, sing long ago the songs of other shores; listen to me, and then in chorus gather all your deep voices as ye pull your oars; from the lone sheiling of the misty island, mountains divide us, and a waste of seas; yet still the blood is strong, the heart is Highland, and we in dreams behold the Hebrides; Fair these broad meads, these hoary woods are grand, but we are exiles from our father's land."

It was a song of the *voyageurs,* and though most of the men who stroked the great fur-brigade canoes were French, in this case we have a keening lament for the lost and misty hills of Scotland.

Washington Irving, the son of an Orkney farmer, wrote two outstanding books on the northwest fur trade: *Astoria* and *The Adventures of Captain Bonneville.* Irving termed the men of Astoria, especially those of Scottish blood, in unflattering phrases: "The swelling and braggart style of these hyperborean nabobs . . . the wintering partners, many of them of good Scottish families, with a score of retainers at their bidding, fancied themselves in the role of Highland chieftains . . . (they were) the lords of the lakes and forests."[7]

One Scot seized the opportunity and turned Irving's phrases to advantage: "Lords of the forests and lakes were they, who came from afar to Hudson's Bay; stalwart of stature, silent and stern, rugged of feature, eager to learn, the ways of the West, the grim Nor'west . . . From Mull of Kintyre and Firth of Clyde, the Border country and Teviot side, The Solway Firth and Isles of the North, Their quest for adventure drove them forth, to the unknown West . . . McKenzie, Campbell, Fraser and Rae are names immortal in Hudson's Bay . . ."[8]

These verses are not so far removed in spirit from those of "Scotish Fielde," published in Bishop Percy's *Reliques* in 1765: "From Orkney that Ile there came a great host, from Galloway a Gay lord, with a great menie, all Scottland thither came, to know their Kings mind . . . such an host of that nation was never seen before, their names were numbered, to nine score thousand, truly by their owne tounge, as it was told after."[9]

The spirit of battle followed the fighting clans to the New World. The battle between the North West Company and the mighty Hudson's Bay Company for control of the fur trade had its counterparts in the bloody clan warfare back home in the Highlands. Interest in the stories of struggle were even found in two French ballads which were translated into English. One was *Lord Selkirk at Fort William* which is a light-hearted spoof listing the names of John McNab, William McGillivray, Kenneth McKenzie, John McLoughlin, and Simon Fraser. All of them were involved in the battle between the two companies. *The Battle of Seven Oaks*, one of the key events in the struggle, is also by Pierre Falcon, and was translated from *La Bataille Des Sept-Chenes*, "We took three Orkney prisoners there, three men from across the sea who'd come to pillage our country."[10]

Scottish ballads, like the songs of the French voyageurs, frequently dealt with medieval themes of chivalry, so the translations were in the proper spirit. As W. Stewart Wallace said, "the names of the North West Company partners sound like a roll call of the clans of Culloden."[11] It is no wonder that the fighting, singing heritage came with them.

Thus when Scots meet on Robert Burns Night, "after the cup goes round" there will be a burst of music — melancholy refrains for the lost glories of Scotland followed by the martial songs of the fighting clans. Sometimes the refrain is ridiculous, such as the famous inscription on the grave stone of "Fair Maiden Lilliard," who fought beside her lover at the Battle of Ancrum Muir, in 1545: "Fair Maiden Lilliard lies under this stane, Little was her stature, but great was her fame; upon the English loons she laid mony thumps, and when her legs were cuttit off, she focht upon her Stumps!"[12] Fortunately, not all are so grim.

When folk songs and ballads migrated from their place of origin, in this case, the British Isles — they changed gradually in tone and character. Historical names lost their meaning and sometimes local names were substituted. "Lord Randal," of Scottish tradition, became "Lord Randolph" in Virginia, where the name meant something. New folk songs were created, arising out of various occupational groups, and differing in this respect from the way in which they were born back in Scotland, where the source was more homogenous regardless of occupation. For example, *The Scot's Lament*, or *The Canadian Boat Song*, as it is sometimes called, came from an environment not strictly Scottish: the French *voyageur* was there, too, singing his own "paddling songs," most of which were versions of the "chansons" of medieval France; there were also English and Irish working in the fur trade posts or along the rivers of the northwest. The musical situation could get even more confusing, when the "Kanakas," men from the Sandwich Islands, were present. Noting Dr. Tolmie's description of a musical evening at Fort McLoughlin in my chapter *Botanizing Scots*, a New Year's celebration marked by songs and dances, from the Scottish reels, *voyageur* songs, Iroquois war dances, to the Sandwich Islanders' version of *Rule Britannia!*

One Scot recalled the Old World tradition as he sailed for America, half-way between the old life and the new: "Forty lads on the open sea, out to work for the HBC . . . tae entertain the folk on board, a song was sung, which was encored, aft in my dreams I hear the roar, as the Hielanders walked off the floor."[13]

Another Scot provided the next bit of the scenario: "Here on a cold and foreign strand, I think of home and native land; of thule, 'mid the ocean's roar, I love her sea-bound cliffy shore. But while I here a stranger roam, though ne'er may I return home, to Shetland's hills, so bleak and bare, yet to my wistful eyes, how fair . . ." Then, in what must be reckoned as a third stage in the period of transition, he suddenly remembers that what he left behind was not really all that marvelous: "I would not care elsewhere to be, no, not beside the tall fir tree, here in this land of liberty . . . for here in this land in which I roam, each man is lord of his own home . . . O all you sons of Thule's soil, who day by day go forth to toil, why not let ambition rise to send you forth to reach the prize, of rightful life and liberty, in this fair land, America."[14]

One Jamie Anderson followed the gold rush to the Fraser River, and commented morosely on how fleeting success can be: "I ken a body made a strike, he looked a little lord; he had a clan of followers amang a needy horde; Whane'er he'd enter a saloon you'd see the barkeep smile — his Lordship's humble servant he, wi'out a thought of guile! A twalmonth passed an' a' is gane, baith friends and brandy bottle; an' noo the puir soul's left alane wi' nocht to wet his throttle!"[15]

While Jamie was "doon," he heard from his sweetheart back home in Scotland: "Your letter cam' by the express, eight shillin's carriage, naethin' less! you maybe like to ken what pay we miners get for ilka day? Jus' two poond sterling, sure as death — it should be four, between us baith — for gin ye count the cost o' livin', there's naethin' left to gang and come on."[16] Despite adversity, he retained a sense of humor, if little else! Jamie's financial concerns serve to remind us of the ancient canards about the proverbial stinginess of the Scot. Several songs have been written about his "closeness wi' the shillin',"[17] but most Scots say it is all English propaganda, and have their peculiar way of getting back at their tormentors. Take two stories and then meet the rebuttal: an Aberdonian went into a shop and bought a suitcase (a small one). The clerk asked, "Shall I wrap it up for you?" And Sandy replied, "Oh, no, thank you, just put the paper and the string inside." Another strange tale has three Scotsmen in church one Sunday, when the minister, speaking for some worthy cause, said that he hoped everyone there would give at least a crown or more. As the collection plate neared their aisle, the three Scots became very nervous. One fainted and the other two carried him out to fresh air! Then, the scurrilous ditty which goes, "here's to the Scotsman, long may he wave! to take a mean chance on the money he'd save, he'd walk to his funeral, or dig his own grave."[18]

To counter this propaganda which (they say) crept north from England, "that tiny island ruled by Scotsmen," such stories as the following were current north of Carlisle: in an English political meeting one of the candidates orated, "I was born an Englishman, I have lived an Englishman, I hope I shall die an Englishman." From the back of the hall, an unmistakable Scottish brogue asked the question, "Mon, hae ye no ambeetion?"

Most of this kind of thinking has found its way into songs and ballads. Northwestern Scots know story after story about the Scot's reputation for stinginess, and most can laugh at them as weapons in the war of words between two ethnic groups who fought for centuries. Nor was the penchant for warfare always limited to verbal blasts. Many a clan went to battle against another clan for some fancied insult. Ask about "the Curse of Scotland," which is the nine of diamonds, based upon its similarity to the arms of the Duke of Argyle, the man who is credited with bringing about the Union with England; or, some believe, the nine of spades, saying that news of a great Scottish defeat was brought to Edinburgh on the back of such a card;[19] or the saying by King Charles I (who lost his head later) "there never was a rebellion in Scotland without either a Campbell or a Dalrymple at the bottom of it"[20] The real cause of rebellion, according to Sir Walter Scott, in his *Tales of a Grandfather*, was "the sense of the habitually insulting and injurious manner in which they were treated by the English . . . as if the representatives of some inferior and subjugated province."[21] Scott is paraphrasing the same Duke of Argyll, but with more sympathy than is implied by "the Curse of Scotland." The proud spirit even comes out in the Scotsman's last words to humanity. Engraved on one stone is the epitaph, "Here lie I, Martin Elginbrod; hae mercy on my soul, Lord God; as I would do, were I Lord God, and Ye were Martin Elginbrod."[22]

One is sorely tempted to stray away from the subject in hand, when one gets into Scottish folklore. We were talking about ballads and folk songs, but for two pages now we have inserted a stream of jokes, sayings, and anecdotes. Perhaps one may be excused by saying that of such stuff were the ballads made. By its very nature, the ballad tells a story, and these were some of the stories!

Ideally, in order to do justice to the subject, one should pack a tape recorder into some of the isolated communities of the northwest, seeking out first-generation Scots who may still retain, through recall and/or performance, a repertoire of the traditional songs. Certain areas of the Pacific Northwest were settled by Scots, and a number still retain that identity. The border counties of Washington and Idaho, the three western Canadian provinces, "pockets" of settlement, such as the Upper Cowlitz, the Skagit, and Skamania, in Washington; descendants of the Red River colonists on Puget Sound and in the Willamette Valley, in Oregon; Mormons of Scottish descent, in southern Idaho; all of these, and more, are fertile fields for "song-catching," as Dorothy Scarborough called a similar mission in the mountains of the southeast.[23]

Here and there, in these isolated settlements, one may surprise a native "Bard," who is composing and performing songs to match his mountains. Two come to mind: Ron McLean, in Winthrop, Washington, a school teacher who back-packs through the Cascades at every opportunity, and entertains hikers at mountain campfires;[24] the other is Rosalie Sorrels of Boise, who has tracked down many ballads and is responsible for a few of her own.[25] Whether or not their songs will become traditional, only time — much time — will tell. In Scotland, it generally took two or three centuries before the songs were absorbed into the folk tradition. But today, with mass communication, especially the pervasive influence of television, who knows? One thing sure, television may be killing off the old songs at a rate faster than such performers as Judy Collins or

Joan Baez can work to preserve them.

I wonder if Woody Guthrie had a Scottish heritage?[26] The name is common in Scotland. Woody spent only a few weeks in the Pacific Northwest, but out of that period came about twenty-eight songs. (The number is a matter of dispute.) In profound ways, Guthrie was "folk," in the bardic tradition. One thing does separate his songs of the northwest from the classical ballad tradition. That was his self-involvement in the verses. A true ballad is supposed to be impersonal, not giving utterance to the mood or feelings of the singer. The singer, according to George Lyman Kittredge (in an introduction to Childs' ballads)[27] does not take sides for or against the *dramatis personae* of the song. He merely tells what happened and what people said, the story existing for its own sake. This explains the rather flattened affect which most ballad-singers present, in an unemotional rendition of the song being sung.

To ask that Woody Guthrie "not take sides" would have been like asking Tom Joad to enlist in a sheriff's posse! Woody would have been the first to disavow a "folk anonymity," since he, like the ancient Scots, often looked upon words as weapons.[28] Guthrie is our clue to the ballad process at work in the northwest. Today folk singers do not hesitate to add or to drop words from his songs, drop a stanza or add a new one, alter rhymes, change names, or to do whatever suits a given occasion.[29] This is the folk process at work. His songs have been used for causes he would have deplored. If the axiom that governs the classic ballad applies, it may be one or two centuries, or, at the least, several generations, before Guthrie's songs have entered the folk tradition. I said that with Guthrie, the folk process is under way already, more remarkable in that his songs were written less than forty years ago. Unfortunately, we will not be around to find out whether or not his songs survive and enter the tradition. Based upon what we know about him and about the songs, his chances for survival seem excellent.

The classic Scottish folk song or ballad is essentially non-religious. In many examples there are invocations of the supernatural, accounts of strange creatures, such as "the great Silkie," tales of revenge beyond the grave, or accounts of bloody battles. "The Twa Corbies," with the mysterious visit to a slain knight by two ravens, is typical. Bleak and without pity, the ballad was collected by Sir Walter Scott for his *Minstrelsy of the Scottish Border*, who for some unfathomable reason, classified it as "a romantic ballad."[30] Romance indeed! The ravens are discussing as to how they shall proceed to dine on the fallen warrier! "Ye'll sit on his white house-bane, and I'll pike out his bonny blue een: wi' ae lock o' his gowden hair, we'll theek our nest when it grows bare . . ." The ballad had what Scott called "a counterpart," in the ballad of *The Three Ravens*.[31] For me, and for all Murdock descendants, the tone is much more sympathetic, for which we render thanks, inasmuch as *The Three Ravens* are on the family coat of arms. Here the knight is rescued by "a fallow doe, as great with yong as she might goe; she lift up his bloudy hed, and kist his wounds that were so red; she got him up upon her backe, and carried him to carthern lake; she buried him before the prime, she was dead herselfe ere even-song time; God send every gentleman, such haukes, such hounds, and such a leman." Ever since I visited Scotland and first heard the story behind the family coat of arms, I have been delighted that young Murdock and his two brothers put arrows through those bloody birds! The ravens had it coming, a just reward for their frustrated cannibalism. But, on the other hand, as an inquiring student might say, the raven was the sacred bird of Woden, the Norse god.[32] By destroying his talisman were the Scots also attempting to efface traces of the ancient Norse invasions? We may never know.

No attempt to destroy ancient rituals and customs, as personified by the classic ballads and folk songs of Scotland, was waged more rigorously than the efforts of the "Covenanters" to wipe out such traditions. The Covenanters were the forerunners of the Presbyterians, described as marked by "earnestness, rugged devotedness, and an almost insane sincerity."[33] The great battles between Church and State which marked the 17th century were prime causes for emigration to the New World. In 1645 the Covenanters defeated forces under the Marquis of Montrose; five years later, the English under Cromwell defeated an army of Covenanters at Dunbar; then, at Bothwell Bridge, the subject of a great ballad, the Covenanters were routed with severe loss of life. The battle of Bothwell Bridge took place in 1679, and the years which followed witnessed many executions of the Covenanter leaders. My mother's family left Scotland in 1687, fleeing Cumloden, which had been granted to them by Robert the Bruce following the battle of Bannockburn in 1314. Cumloden, in Galloway, was in the heart of the Covenanting country. They may have been fleeing for their lives, though I have no evidence to support this. In any case, America offered a refuge, as it has for countless refugees since. Scott's *Minstrelsy of the Scottish Border* gives a lengthy account of the circumstances which led to the battle of Bothwell Bridge. He refers to "the more moderate class of Presbyterians," specifically to Alexander Gordon, of Earlstoun, the hero of the ballad. Gordon's eventual escape from execution is one of the greatest adventure stories in Scottish history.[34] "Alang the brae, beyond the brig, mony brave man lies cauld and still; but lang we'll mind, and sair we'll rue, the bloddy battle of

Bothwell Hill."[35]

Not all Scots were Presbyterians, a statement so simple-minded that most Scots would laugh. The other side of the story, told by those unsympathetic to the cause, or the adherents of the Church of England or the Church of Rome, is symbolized in a rare tome called *Scots Presbyterian Eloquence Displayed, or Their manner of Teaching and Preaching exposed . . . interspersed with Some genuine and curious Adventures on different Occasions.* The edition I had access to was the eleventh, published in London in 1767, many years after Presbyterianism was firmly established in Scotland. The book is pure folklore, filled with legends, tales, proverbial sayings, some suspect "history," even a little poetry. The author was anonymous, writing under the obvious pseudonym, "Jacob Curate."[36] At the end is appended "A Short Catechism for the Instruction of Young and Old." Some of the questions and answers are hilarious: "Wherefore do not the Presbyterians sing glory to God on high?" *Answer*: "Because that was a song of Angels, made upon Yool-day; and they are not for Christmas carrols." *Question*: "What do the Presbyterians think of the government in heaven?" *Answer*: "They think it too prelatical; for the word Archangel sounds like Archbishop, and they wonder that the Angels made not a Covenant against the Archangels in heaven, as the Presbyterians made against the Archbishops on earth." *Question*: "Why do the Presbyterians give the title of saints to the rebels that died at Pentland-hills and Bothwell bridge, and yet will not give the title of saints to any of the Apostles?" *Answer*: "Because the Apostles never subscribed the Solemn League and Covenant, and never rose in arms against the King." There is much more, but this will do for now. As William Lyon Phelps said, upon the occasion of his appointment to be Literary Editor for *Esquire* magazine, "It will probably give equal consternation to the godly and the ungodly." Enough, therefore, of the "Short Catechism." You may find the book yourself if you want to pursue the subject.

"Repent, brethren, the word exhorts us to duty." The unknown author begs us to consider the letters of the word *repent*, and what they stand for: readily, earnestly, presently, early, nationally, thoroughly, again, rarely, elegantly, prettily, evenly, neatly, and, finally, tightly. All, he said, applied to the Scottish Covenanter. He concludes with what he calls "A Doggrel on Dominie Anderson," an amusing rhyme which I will not inflict on mixed company.[37]

Psalm-singing should not play any part in a chapter on ballads and folk songs. *The Old Hundred*, "Praise God from Whom all blessings flow" and the other hymns which became associated with Presbyterianism, came late to the religious scene, since all singing could get out of hand. But "making a joyful noise unto the Lord" finally came into its own, as any of today's Presbyterian hymnals will show. Under new sponsorship, the singing tradition of Scotland lives on. As for Scotland, Presbyterian church government, established in 1592 by Royal Act, was again recognized by Parliament in 1689. Perhaps my family left too soon!

The folk ballad tradition (to depart now from religious songs) lived on when the Scots emigrated to America. Sometimes the Scot or his children became the heroes of the ballads which bloomed in the new land. With apologies for a personal note, such was the case with my own family. I have traced four folk songs which relate to our family history — two for my mother's side, which are applicable, because they were Scots; two to my father's family, which was French and Dutch. The two of Scottish derivation need only concern us here.[38]

The first, in point of time, was the ballad *Joshua Stevens*. The name is misspelled, and should read "Stephens." The story of the ballad is of the murder of young Joshua Stephens by two Indians named "Sundown" and "George Curlyeye." It happened in about 1823, in the Canisteo Valley, near Hornell, New York, where I first saw the light of day. The story of the event appears in a *History of the Settlement of Steuben County, New York*, published in 1853. The murder led to a trial at Bath, New York, then and now the county seat. According to Guy McMaster, a fellow Scot who wrote the account, "the affair created a great sensation, and the trial was attended by a large concourse of people. Red Jacket (a famous Indian leader) and other prominent chiefs were present. The evidence against the prisoners was of a strong character, but they were acquitted. After this event the Indians became shy and evacuated the county, and never returned again except in straggling bands." I won't give the entire ballad here, since, like their Scottish prototypes, the American ballads sometimes run to inordinate length. The story the ballad tells is typical of the kind of sensational event that always brought forth the talents of some provincial bard. "From Squawky Hill two Indians came, to Bennett's Creek to hunt for game; The Indians names we can't deny, were Sundown and George Curlyeye." The song moves through three stanzas to set the scene, then, "He went from home one afternoon, his oxen in the woods to find; the Indians shot him in the side, which caused his death can't be denied . . . 'twas the next morning he was found, lying near the road upon the ground; behold poor Joshua, slim and tall, and in him lay a savage ball" . . . with each dot representing another lugubrious stanza. An inquest was called, his widow wept, his children cried, his "feeble father raised his moan to think the Indians killed his son . . ." Bennett's Creek, the scene of the crime, is where I used to play with Eddie Bennett and other classmates, when a boy in Hornell. My aunt, Marian Stephens, still lives in Hornell, and her son, Lynn, in Beaver Dam, 155 years after the sad event celebrated by the ballad.

Somewhat further west (two thousand miles further), "Captain Murdock" slipped into the folklore of the Latter Day Saints. He was John Riggs Murdock, the son of John Murdock who went west with Joseph Smith from upstate New York. He served as wagon-master for the Mormon trains snaking their way west to Utah. The ballad, *Captain Murdock*, sometimes called *Captain John*, is a whip-cracking, teeth-jolting commemoration of that service to the pioneer Mormons. The song is well-known in Utah and the Rocky Mountain west today. As with many Scots' ballads, *Captain Murdock* celebrates the exploits of a man of action and derring-do.[39]

My guess is that anyone who cares to go back far enough in history can find such traditions in family history. There are undoubtedly Scots in the northwest who can tell similar stories. The fun will be in digging into the local history of those settlements which offered refuge from Scotland's wars, "Clearances," and religious persecution, together with the opportunity and the freedom to grow in the new land of Promise.

What did we learn from all of this? First, as stated in the introduction, that "the sweetest songs are those of saddest memories," which certainly applied to the ballads and songs the Scot brought with him; second, that the act of leaving the homeland was itself an act of great sadness; third, that his arrival and first months in the New World were lonely and nostalgic; finally, and this is the best of all, that after he was acclimated, he could once more sing songs of adventure or heroism about events in which he may have taken an active part. Compare the two songs which follow. The first is the usual lament for the home he is leaving behind: "Farewell, farewell, my native hame, thy lonely glens an' heathclad mountains; farewell thy fields of storied fame, thy leafy shaws an' sparklin' fountains; Nae mair I'll climb the Pentlands' steep, nor wander by the Esk's clear river, I seek a home far o'er the deep, my native land, farewell forever." This is *The Scottish Emigrant's Farewell*, published in Edinburgh in the early nineteenth century."[40]

Now (looking back to the song quoted earlier in this chapter), he has arrived, and writes home to others who hesitate to follow: "I would not care elsewhere to be . . . here in this land of liberty . . . for here in this land in which I roam, each man is lord of his own home." From here on, the "sweet, sad songs" of Scotland begin to fade in memory, only to be recalled when New World Scots get together, to shed a sentimental tear over the changes wrought by time and distance.

60

Chapter Ten

Women: liberated or otherwise

ROSS

Northwest historians have not dealt fairly with the substantial contributions of women. The record has generally been compiled by men, which may explain the gap. As a result, it is very difficult to trace the careers of the women who made a significant impact upon our regional history. This situation is beginning to change now, and historians may continue what was begun by such writers as Frances Fuller Victor, Abigail Scott Duniway, Dorothy Johansen, Margaret Ormsby, and others.[1]

Some women left diaries, letters, reminiscences, or articles, often published in obscure places. From these it is possible to translate scattered facts into something near trustworthy biography. But when the field is narrowed to include only women of Scottish heritage, the task becomes monumental. When we choose a few notable names to write about here the choice must be symbolic, accepting the lamentable fact that where a few sources survived, most of the others are silent. The stories of hundreds of deserving women will probably remain unknown, or preserved only in family tradition.

It would be nice to be able to record that the first Caucasian woman in northwest history was a Scot. She wasn't. Two names occur — Frances Hornby Trevor Barkley, who came with her husband, Captain Charles William Barkley, in 1787, but whose diary is surrounded by mystery;[2] Jane Barnes, brought to Fort George by Chief Factor Donald McTavish on the *Isaac Todd*, after the British took over Astoria during the War of 1812. Jane was identified as a pretty barmaid from Plymouth, England, and is the first white woman of record on the Columbia.[3] Her stay at the Fort stirred up all kinds of trouble. She reputedly dropped McTavish in favor of another Scot, Alexander Henry, in the first few weeks of her stay. Shortly after, both McTavish and Henry, plus five other men, were drowned when a boat capsized in sight of Fort Goerge. The son of Chief Concomly, "painted and decked in all the glory of a prince's vestments," offered to marry Jane, with a gift of one hundred sea otter skins to boot. Jane turned down the bribe and left shortly after on a ship bound for Canton.[4]

So, while we cannot say that the first white woman to appear on the northwest scene was Scottish, we at least acknowledge that she got there because of a Scottish invitation! Poor Donald McTavish did not live long enough to appreciate her acceptance.

As with Mrs. Barkley and Jane Barnes, it was the fur trade which did bring the first women from Scotland to the northwest. Many of the Scots traders had returned to Scotland to marry, others, in a fewer cases, sent for them to join them on the frontier. But, for every fur trader who brought a young bride from Scotland, there were many times the number who married Indian women.[5] Many of the native women were great helpmates, some the offspring of Indian leaders like Chief Concomly, leader of the Chinooks on the lower Columbia. Concomly met two historic expeditions — Lewis and Clark, in 1805, and the Astor party, in 1811. He had several daughters who married fur traders, one being Princess Raven who wed Archibald MacDonald and bore the famous Ranald MacDonald, about whom we learn more in another chapter.[6] When the Princess and the Scot were married, Chief Concomly carpeted the path from the bridal canoe, drawn up on the river bank, all the way to the gates of Fort George! The royal carpet was of sea-otter skins, a veritable fortune in furs, and represented the Princess' dowry.

Some of the most respected names in northwest history were associated with these "fur trade marriages" — Dr. John McLoughlin, Charles Ross, Edward Ermatinger, and many others. Their descendants have been movers and shakers in our regional history. But, unfortunately, few of the Indian wives were literate, therefore there are few written records from their point of view. The fur trade journals tell their story, but only in part. We would treasure written accounts by the women themselves.

The appearance of European wives at the fur trade posts made for difficult social relationships for those men of the posts who had Indian or mixed-blood wives. The introduction of a kind of caste system into what had been the rather free and easy social life on the frontier created complications, and, in some cases, great animosities. Sylvia Van Kirk explored the subject at length in an article in the Hudson's Bay Company magazine, *The Beaver,* titled *Women and the Fur Trade* (*The Beaver,* Winter 1972). I recommend it highly.

The women who moved from the rigid confines of a class structure in Europe to the beginning of another in the northwest fur trade may have adjusted rather easily to the new system. After all, the sketch of a young bride learning to adapt to life at a wilderness fur trade post was only part of the larger picture of cultural confrontation. The collision of native, or Indian, folkways with European, or "civilized" customs, was involved.

A fairly typical account of the process is the diary of Frances Simpson, the wife of Sir George Simpson, Governor of the Hudson's Bay Company in North America from 1821 to 1860.[7] She was the daughter of Geddes Mackenzie Simpson, a Scottish merchant who had first employed George Simpson as a clerk in his London counting-house. At the time she married George, Frances was 18 years old, while he, a 20 year veteran of the fur trade, was 43. Her diary began with the trip from England to Canada, and includes the sketch of a transcontinental journey in Hudson's Bay fur brigade canoes, from Montreal to the Red River settlement in western Canada.

The story is one of hardship and adventure, in about equal parts. The author's delighted account of the customs of the new country through which they traveled brightens the story. As Governor in command of a vast wilderness empire, Simpson visited the trading posts under his command from one end of the continent to the other. His young wife described how he would arouse the party each morning before dawn, calling "levé, levé, levé" to waken the sleeping French voyageurs. Following a hurried breakfast, they all boarded the great canoes and resumed the westward journey. The songs of the voyageurs delighted the young Scottish bride, and were a great relief during the tedious passages between the next bay or portage.

The Governor was a fanatic for speed. Grace Lee Nute, who edited the diary of Frances Simpson, was appalled at the demands which Simpson made of his crews. Editor Nute made a test journey by canoe from the Maligne River to Lac La Croix, with many rapids en route. Her 20th century party of paddlers took two days to complete the trip. Simpson's party performed the feat in just six hours!

The Simpson party reached Lac La Pluie Fort on Rainy River after several accidents to the canoe, and after drenching rains. Frances records her joy at the hospitable reception at the post. The visit lasted only five hours, but the young girl must have left a lasting impression on the men at the post. Several months after her visit, they rechristened the post as "Fort Frances," honoring the pretty young Scot who had graced their company one gloomy June day three months before.

On another occasion, Frances records with obvious satisfaction the names of some of the men who greeted their party when they arrived at a Hudson's Bay Company post on Lake Superior. Her diary recalls the salute of cannon and the reception by the chief factors and Company clerks who had journeyed there from other posts just to greet the Governor and his new bride. The names she cited were George Keith, Alexander Christie, John McBean, Nicol Finlayson — all fellow Scots. What "a security blanket" for the wilderness frontier! In one sense, at least, she had never left home.

Frances Simpson's diary is a delightful report of what it meant to one Scottish girl to travel from Scotland by long sea voyage to America; the sometimes tedious but always challenging experience of transcontinental travel, meeting new scenes and people in a strange, new land. Reactions to her first confrontation with the culture of various Indian tribes were fairly representative. Her narrative seems to glow with a kind of delighted inner laughter, with descriptions of the springtime beauties they encountered along the way alternating with breathless accounts of dangers met and passed. And if it glows, why not? She was, after all, a young bride on a honeymoon trip which few have equalled since.

Just thirty years after Frances Simpson made her memorable journey, another young Scot came to western America, met and mastered the frontier, and, God be thanked, made a record of her experiences.[8] She was Susan Moir, born in Colombo, Ceylon, the daughter of Stratton Moir, a Scottish plantation owner. Her father died when Susan was only four years old, and her mother took Susan, her brother, and two sisters, back to England to live. During their stay in England the little family frequently visited Aberdeen, where her father had graduated as a Master of Arts in 1829. Then, her mother, still a young woman, married again, a Scottish gentleman named Thomas Glennie. The Fraser River gold excitement was at its peak in western Canada in 1860, and Glennie wanted to go. Not about to be left alone again with her small children, Susan's mother packed them along, with the exception of Susan's brother who remained in London as a banking apprentice. To British Columbia they emigrated, arriving on the west coast just shortly after the election of Abraham Lincoln. The people of California, where they spent two weeks resting before sailing for Victoria aboard the *Otter*, a Hudson's Bay Company ship, were all agog about the possibility of the South seceding from the Union. One southern gentleman named Selim Waterberry protested to Susan that the South should be reimbursed by the federal government if they were forced to give up their slaves.

En route to British Columbia, the boat stopped at Portland after making its way up the Columbia with the mail. Susan was not impressed by the frontier city, commenting that its orchards were more impressive than its houses. They proceeded immediately to Victoria where her step-father presented letters of introduction to James Douglas, a fellow Scot who was now Governor of Vancouver Island. Douglas advised Mr. Glennie to go to Hope, the head of navigation on the Fraser River. He predicted that Hope and the surrounding area had a bright future and suggested that Mr. Glennie "take up land" there. Accepting the advice, they again boarded the *Otter*, sailing to New Westminster on the mainland where they changed ships for the trip up the Fraser River to Hope.

Susan celebrated her fifteenth birthday as they landed at Hope, which she described as "a charming, busy little place . . . nestling in the mountains and Ogilvie's Peak towering above it." There began a new life for the transplanted Scottish family. Her reminiscences tell of the necessary adjustments to frontier living, adventures in riding horseback on the Hope-

Similkameen road, and of how she helped her mother to start a school. In 1868 she married John Fall Allison, who had been in the California gold rush, then had come to the Fraser River diggings in 1859. When the mining became hydraulic and personal prospecting no longer paid off, he went into the cattle business on an 160 acre claim in the Similkameen district. There he eked out a living, supplemented by contracts for building roads and improving trails for the government. By 1866, with a partner named Hayes, he had accumulated a large stock of cattle. But, the mining fever subsided, and the "Big Bend" rush of that year petered out, leaving him with the necessity of driving the cattle over the Hope Mountains to market at New Westminster. It was on one of these cattle drives that Allison made arrangements to marry Susan Moir.

When Susan started on her honeymoon trip over the Hope Mountains, riding side-saddle, she was only the second Caucasian woman to make the dangerous journey. The other woman, a Mrs. Marston, in 1860, was so terrified that she dismounted and walked most of the way from Hope to Similkameen! Susan was exhilarated when she began the journey and she was not frightened, having confidence in the Indian packers who led the train. They made the trip safely and she set up housekeeping for her new husband at Similkameen. The only neighbors were the Indians. Her husband was away frequently for long periods of time during the cattle drives which they counted on for income.

Susan loved the color and adventure of the new land. One of her trips took her to Lake Okanogan, riding horseback over rugged and dangerous terrain. Susan's diary recounts the thrill of her first encounter with Lake Okanagan. Silence, a deep calm on the lake, and the reflection of the mountains on the unruffled waters cast a kind of spell. Even the Indians who had accompanied the party were awed, and all rode in silence through rye grass shoulder-high.

The party made camp, had a good supper, and put the children to bed. She said, "I joined the story tellers," who included Saul, the Indian chief, and Johnny McDougal, a half-caste trail-driver. The conversation turned to the mythical monster of the Lake — "Ogopogo," as the Indians called the legendary sea serpent of Okanagan. McDougal recalled how he drove his horses toward the Narrows to cross over, as he frequently did when hunting. It had always been his custom to take a chicken or a small pig to be dropped into the Lake as he approached the middle — a kind of living sacrifice to appease the strange creature which occupied the depths. This time he had overlooked the sacrifice, and as he towed the horses behind on a long rope, something suddenly pulled them down under the water. Johnny said his canoe would have been next to go under if he had not cut the rope and hurried to reach the shore. The team of horses was never found. Susan said that this story, and others like it "had a strange charm for me."

The legend of Ogopogo could have been lifted completely from Scotland's Loch Ness monster folklore. It wasn't, since the Indians knew of the sea serpent on Lake Okanogan for centuries before the coming of the white man. The setting of the glacial lake, the high surrounding mountains — the theory that an arm of the ancient sea had been blocked off during the glacial age — all were completely reminiscent of the Loch Ness setting in the Highlands of Scotland. That an ancient creature from Mesozoic time could have been trapped in a blocked arm of the sea made perfect sense to the young Scot. The stories' "strange charm" was in keeping with her Celtic heritage.

As for the "Big Men," or Sasquatch, stories by the Indians, the gigantic, furry monster was first reported by David Thompson in his *Narrative of His Exploration in Western Canada*, 1784-1812. That account contains a mention of a Sasquatch sighted in the rugged interior of British Columbia. You can get an argument today anytime the question is raised by Scot or non-Scot. Is he or isn't he?

In the appendix to Susan's published journal, *A Pioneer Gentlewoman in British Columbia: the Recollections of Susan Allison,* the editor, Margaret A. Ormsby, included a short story written by Susan which drew upon tales she had heard from the Indians. The story is told by an ancient Indian who once encountered a Sasquatch while on a hunting trip into the mountains. Surprised while sleeping, the Sasquatch picked him up and carried him to a cave which he shared with another "Big Man." Held prisoner for a long time, they allowed him to go fishing and hunting with them, while always guarding him from escape. They treated him kindly, displaying emotions common to humans, such as sympathy for pain. The old Indian described "the high, shrieking whistle as of the north wind" by which they communicated, and "the vile, suffocating odor" they carried. Interesting to note: every description of a Sasquatch-sighting today here in the Pacific Northwest, mentions the same characteristics.

Eventually the captive escaped to freedom, on a night when the great rock which was always rolled to block the cave exit was not perfectly in place, thereby leaving room for the Indian to slip through to the outside and freedom. Ever after this experience, even though back among his own people, he said that the shrill shrieking whistle of the north wind was a dreaded sound, "for in it I hear the whistle of the 'Big Men' . . ."

When his listeners questioned him as to whether or not the "Big Men" were spirits, or whether they ever die as Indians do, the old man replied, "Who can tell, my child? No one knows. There are strange things in these mountains."

Susan remembered that there were many strange and unexplained things back home in the mountains of Scotland, too. The northwest frontier only supplied a new setting. Being half a Scot, I half believe the stories myself.

A very good indication of just how far women have come is a story from my family history. Samuel Murdock was one of the second generation of Murdocks in America, his father, Robert, having emigrated from Scotland to Plymouth in 1687. He was born in Roxbury, Massachusetts, in 1698, his mother being Hannah Stedman, whose parents had come from England to Scituate in 1636.[10]

In 1725 Samuel married Submit Throop in Lebanon, Connecticut. Submit was the daughter of Dan and Deborah Throop. The Throop family of Connecticut has always claimed descent from Adrian Scroop, famed for his part in the arrest and execution of Charles I, of England. After the Restoration the name was changed to Throop and the family fled to America to escape the wrath of the reinstated monarchy.

Samuel joined many of his relatives who migrated from Newton, Massachusetts, to Connecticut. There he bought land and was admitted to the church with his wife in 1726. In 1735 he bought one hundred and twenty-two acres of land, and in 1736 ninety more adjoining at Windham, to which he and his family moved the following year.

Samuel did well in Windham where he was admitted to the church in 1738. Connecticut Colonial Records give his commission as "Captain of the Troop of Horse of the Fifth Regiment" in 1741. He served seven times in the Connecticut General Assembly as Deputy for Windham. He died, full of honors, in 1769, and his will is a classic, which, after all, is the point of all this. The will divides his property, the homestead being left to his youngest son Eliphalet. It contained the following provision for his wife:

"I give and bequeath unto my dearly beloved wife Submit a good riding jade and furniture and two milch cows, six good sheep and increase and twelve pounds of flax yearly and the use of my negro girl during her natural life and have the use of the upright part of my house and also the use of the middle room as she may have occasion and cellar as much as she needs and Wood at the Door cut as much as she wants and well as she wants. And Priviledge of the outbuildings as much as she wants and Liberty to pass and repass as she has occasion. And to have six bushels of wheat, four of Rye and ten bushels of Indian Corn yearly & Ten score pound of Pork and Sixty pound of Beef and some of all sorts as is laid up in the house; and cyder and Beer as she has occasion for herself and Friends & her proportion of the Poultry as shall be on the Farm. And all my Indoor Goods & Utensils for house keeping excepting what I shall hereafter dispose of in this my Last Will & Testament. And to have her creatures kept well, Winter and Summer." — dated December 1767, signed by Samuel Murdock.[11] The will also named his brother-in-law, Dan Throop, as executor.

Can you see today's emancipated woman putting up with such nonsense? The old Scottish customs, grafted onto American colonial custom, were iron-clad indeed. If the will was, as the family historian put it, "a model of conjugal care," it was also a good example of what women would fight against for the next two hundred years!

A pioneer woman.

George Simpson

Drawing by Andrea Lorig

Susan Moir Allison

Chapter Eleven

Botanizing Scots

KENNEDY

While working in the Pacific Northwest four Scots made lasting contributions to world science: Archibald Menzies, David Douglas, William Fraser Tolmie and William D. Brackenridge. Tolmie and Menzies were physicians. Douglas and Brackenridge were professional botanists. When dealing with scientists the list could be expanded to include George Davidson, the geographer, John Muir, the naturalist, and Meredith Gairdner, but space prohibits. (See *Fifty Scots* at the end of the book.)

Archibald Menzies

Archibald Menzies was the scion of a noted Highlands clan. Born in Weems, Perthshire, he was graduated from the University of Edinburgh from which he received a degree in medicine and qualified as a surgeon. As a surgeon attached to the *Discovery*, Captain George Vancouver's flagship, Menzies visited the northwest coast in 1792. He ascended the Columbia River with Lieutenant Broughton who named an island in the river after him. The name was changed later to Hayden Island. While on Puget Sound Menzies described many plants and trees new to world botany, including the tree later to be called the Douglas fir. Henry Wagner, bibliographer of the northwest exploration, called Menzies' journal of the Vancouver Expedition the finest report to emerge from the famed voyage of 1792.[1] The original journal is a prized holding in the British Museum. The part of the journal dealing with the visit to Puget Sound was edited and published in 1923.[2] The entire journal has never been published complete and certainly should be. Its survival is somewhat miraculous inasmuch as Vancouver demanded its surrender, as he had ordered all diaries and journals to be turned in before the voyage ended. Menzies refused on the grounds that he represented the Royal Horticultural Society. Vancouver, of course, intended to use such documents as grist for his own published journals and reports. You might say that, in a sense, Vancouver won, inasmuch as the official reports were published whereas Menzies' journal has yet to see complete publication.

David Douglas

The Washington State Historical Society presents its "David Douglas Award" to individuals who have made important contributions to northwest history. Douglas deserved the honor, if any of the people of Scots descent did. In three trips to America he added over one thousand plants to the botanical list of his time. Seeds and cuttings of many of these were grown and distributed by the Royal Horticultural Society, his patron, to all parts of the world. It is not just for seeds and cuttings, however, that he is honored by the Society. Instead, it is for the remarkable explorations he carried out alone throughout the northwestern wilderness, and for the equally remarkable journals in which he told his story, that he is saluted.[3]

When David Douglas arrived at Fort Vancouver in 1824 he was greeted and entertained by his fellow Scot, Dr. John McLoughlin. Being at the end of a long journey through the rugged wilderness when he arrived, his clothing was in shreds. McLoughlin gave him a suit of bright red Royal Stewart tartan to replace the tatters. A home away from home, in some respects.

David Douglas was born in the small village of Scone in Perthshire, Scotland.[4] His father was a stonemason, and David was the second son in a family of six. As early as ten years of age, he was learning the fundamentals of gardening. Occasionally he met botanists who had traveled to the Scottish Highlands, and he listened with fascination as they told of their adventures in collecting. These experiences, plus opportunity to work in some fine gardens, whetted his appetite for science and adventure. He was admitted to study at the Botanical Garden in Glasgow.

After several botanical excursions to the Hebrides and into the Highlands, Douglas was picked for special training in London. He was being recognized for his field work by the Royal Horticultural Society who saw promise in the youth. He was expected to prepare for a collecting trip to China but, because relations between China and Great Britain were tenuous at that time, he was dispatched instead to America. He spent a few months collecting specimens on the Atlantic coast, with some fine examples of trees and plants to ship back to England. It was 1823 and Douglas was twenty-four years of age.

In 1824 he sailed again for America on the Hudson's Bay Company brig, the *William and Anne*, bound for the Northwest Coast. The ship coasted South America en route and the young botanist was able to pursue his collecting at various ports of call. He was fascinated by the luxuriant orchid plants at Rio de Janeiro. But when he arrived at Fort Vancouver, on the Columbia, his real work began. His journal, painstaking account that it was, records some of his first reactions to the northwestern wilderness, a region which today has many botanical specimens named either by him or for him. The most familiar name to us is, of course, the Douglas fir, upon which the northwest's leading industry is built.

His journal shows a man in absolute tune with the universe. Here he writes from the Grand Rapids on the Columbia, about a day's journey by canoe from Fort Vancouver: "The scenery is grand beyond description. The high mountains are covered with pines of several kinds, some of great magnitude, with their lofty, wide-spreading branches loaded with snow, while a rainbow stretches over the vapor formed by the agitated waters, which rush with furious speed over the shattered rocks and through the deep channel of the stream, producing a melancholy though pleasing echo through the still and wooded valley, where the vivid green of the Pine contrasts agreeably with the reflection of the snow."[5]

Accustomed to traveling great distances alone, enduring the privations and what he called, in his journal, "the miseries" of wilderness travel, Douglas was still able to visit fellow Scots at the great fur-trade posts. Arriving at the Red River colony, founded by his fellow countryman, the Earl of Selkirk, he spent a month as the guest of Chief Factor Donald McKenzie. McKenzie's hospitable warmth appears in a sketch by James Hargrave, an HBC accountant at York Factory.[6] Writing to Cuthbert Cumming, another Scot who moved from the North West Company to Hudson's Bay Company service, Hargrave appended this amusing description of McKenzie: "Your old Bourgeois is as jolly and plump as ever — rolling about in his inexhaustible good humour, happy himself — and making everyone happy about him . . . it would do your heart good to see him deciding cases ensconced in his elbow chair, covered with a buffalo robe, and crowned with the very identical broad scotch bonnet that he used to sport of yore. Titles and dignities make no change either on his outer or inner man. The same ample suit of grey the same piles of socks — and leggins as capacious as a pemican Bag still decorate his visible and material parts. To sum up all he is, as you used to call him, Sir John Falstaff."

All was not always "malt and cheese," however. Bancroft's *History of British Columbia* tells of Douglas' visit to Fort Kamloop: "It was there the company's officer in command, Samuel Black, challenged his brother Scot and guest, David Douglas, the wandering botanist, to fight a duel, because the blunt visitor one night, while over his rum and dried salmon, had stigmatized the honorable fur-traders as not possessing a soul above a beaver skin. But the enthusiastic pupil of Hooker preferred to fight another day, and so took his departure next morning unharmed."[7]

Douglas returned to England and honors from the Royal Horticultural Society for his many additions to botanical science. But, in 1829, he set sail for the second trip to the Northwest Coast. Because he learned that Indian tribal wars had the Oregon interior in turmoil, he instead journeyed south to California. He visited the Monterey Peninsula where one account labels him as "Doctor" because he had set the author's broken arm, and did it capably.[8] He climbed into the Sierra, along the coastal headlands, through valleys and over mountain ranges collecting as he went.

From California, Douglas sailed to the Sandwich Islands, where from Honolulu he was able to ship home to England his California botanical collection. After the briefest visit to the Island, much marred by the rheumatism he had contracted on the Northwest Coast, he returned to the Columbia River. From thence he went north to the, for him, unexplored area of British Columbia. His canoe was wrecked in the turbulent Fraser River and he lost most of his precious notes, a scientific and historical tragedy since he never found time to rewrite them from memory.

Finally, in 1833, he returned again to Hawaii. This time he climbed Mauna Kea, Mauna Loa, and traveled to the volcano at Kilauea. One of the papers that Douglas wrote for the Royal Horticultural Society was termed *Volcanoes in the Sandwich Islands*. One of the plants he discovered, "the Silver Sword," was later named for him. On his visit to Hawaii, the "Big Island," Douglas commented in a letter to England about seeing wild cattle, the descendants of those brought originally to the islands by Captain George Vancouver, some forty years earlier. The letter may have been prophetic. On his final climb into the mountains, on land where the great Parker Ranch is now located, Douglas fell into a deep pit which had been dug by the natives for the purpose of trapping the wild cattle. The pit already held a trapped bullock. The enraged beast gored and trampled Douglas to death. He was only thirty-five years old when he died.[9]

His body was returned by native canoe to Honolulu. He was buried in the little missionary cemetery next to Kawaiahao Church. The grave is unmarked, although the site was pointed out to members of the Wilkes Expedition which visited the island six years after his death.[10] Several years later, a plaque bearing a Latin inscription honoring Douglas was shipped from England by the Royal Horticultural Society. Originally affixed to an iron gate to the cemetery, the fading plaque was moved years later inside the church. Beside it now hangs a supplementary plaque, also sent from England, with an English translation of the original Latin inscription.

In the Hawaii State Archives there are a number of contemporary accounts of the last rites for David Douglas. One relates how a large guard of British sailors and marines joined the funeral procession, men from a naval ship which happened to be in port at the time. The British consul and high Hawaiian officials were also in attendance at the services and interment near present Kawaiahao Church, now known as the Westminster Abbey of the Islands.[11]

William Fraser Tolmie

Tolmie came to the Pacific Northwest on behalf of the Hudson's Bay Company, arriving in 1833 by way of Cape Horn and the Sandwich Islands. Reporting for duty to Dr. John McLoughlin, he was ordered on to Fort Nisqually, on lower Puget Sound. The fort was under construction and Tolmie took charge of the building operations. Though Tolmie was supposed to proceed on to Fort McLoughlin, on Millbanke Sound, after he had familiarized himself with affairs at Fort Nisqually, an injury sustained by one of the employees at the post required his attention for an extended period. The delay gave him an opportunity to explore the area, particularly Mount Rainier which loomed on the horizon, presenting a great challenge to the young physician.[12]

As Tolmie records in his diary, he recruited five Indians to accompany him, and set out to explore, and, as he put it, "to botanize" in the neighborhood of the mighty mountain. The little party was not really equipped for such a trip. As a result, they endured much suffering which might have been avoided, had they been properly provisioned. Sleeping without cover in downpours of rain, crossing icy rivers without adequate boots or clothing, they finally reached the summit of what is now called "Tolmie's Peak." From this point they had a sweeping view of Mount Rainier, but it was as far as Tolmie could persuade his Indian guides to go. Their superstitious beliefs about the spirit who lived above the timberline forbade their climbing higher.

Tolmie discovered many plants growing on the mountain and in the area nearby which today bear his name. Despite his inability to complete the climb to the true summit of Rainier, the trip paid off scientifically. He was able to collect bird specimens which were unknown to him, such as a Warbler which was later named in his honor by J. K. Townsend, another naturalist (*Oporonis tolmei*).

Though thousands of miles from home now, Tolmie found many Scottish customs in practice on the far northwest frontier. He described his arrival at Fort McLoughlin the Christmas following his Nisqually trip. "Passed the evening very agreeably. Sang several old Scotch ditties and the other gentlemen also tuned their pipes." Tolmie drank "Mountain Dew" along with the rest of them, but claims that he was the only one who awoke the next morning without a headache![13]

But the New Year's celebration which followed one week later was *really* an ethnic mix: "The men after breakfast visited us in the dining hall and after the compliments of the season received a couple of drams. In the evening they assembled in the same apartment and danced with great vivacity till 10 to vocal music. Manson and I danced several reels.

The Canadians possess a natural ease of manner equally remote from the 'free and aisy' of the Emerald Isle and the sheepishness so characteristic of the Sawnee. They sung several paddling songs. Our two Iroquois danced the war dance of their tribe with great spirit, and the Sandwich Islanders sung *Rule Britannia* tolerably well. They all seemed to enjoy themselves highly." As well they might! Here were Scottish Highland reels, French-Canadian voyageur songs, Indian war-dances, capped by the Hawaiians who topped the entire performance with a salute to British imperialism!

Tolmie served at Fort Vancouver from 1836 until 1841, at which time he was given permission to return home for a visit. It took him three months and twelve days to make the trip from Fort Vancouver overland to York Factory, in eastern Canada, by Hudson's Bay Company canoes, afoot, or on snowshoes. He sailed from York Factory to London. During his stay in Europe he was able to take a short course in medicine in Paris. He also managed to study languages, his lectures being in French, and by swapping language lessons with visiting Spanish. His lifelong interest in languages was reflected in studies of the various Indian dialects when he returned to Puget Sound. His fluency in French was particularly helpful in dealing with the French *engages* of the Company. Later on, collaborating with Dr. George Dawson, he would compile a comparative dictionary of Indian languages in British Columbia.[14]

As superintendent of the Nisqually Farms of the Puget Sound Agricultural Company, an arm of the Hudson's Bay Company, Tolmie remained at Fort Nisqually until 1859. Then, thirteen years after the Oregon boundary settlement, he moved to Victoria where he was placed in charge of Company farms on Vancouver Island. He was also appointed one of the three members of the Board of Management of the Hudson's Bay Company.

Doctor Tolmie retired in 1870, after decades of unique contributions which covered an amazing range. Physician and surgeon, botanist, linguist, educator, member of the legislature of British Columbia, he was also a patient negotiator in the final settlement of the claims of the Hudson's Bay Company in the United States. He displayed great patience with incoming American settlers, despite repeated provocations, as some correspondence in an earlier chapter shows.

The last entry in Tolmie's published diary is a rather poignant account about a return visit to Puget Sund after a lapse of nearly forty years. He spent one night visiting his old friend, Ezra Meeker, at his home in Puyallup.[15] The two old men had much to recall, having kept up only a desultory correspondence during Tolmie's long residence in Victoria. Tolmie also visited James G. Swan, of Port Townsend, a kindred soul who shared many interests in Indian history and customs, and who was the first collector in this region for the Smithsonian Institution.[16] The last night of his visit he spent in the new and luxurious Tacoma Hotel, a marvelous change from the rough pioneering life he experienced at Fort Nisqually when he first arrived on Puget Sound a half-century before, a young medical graduate from Glasgow just barely twenty-one years old.

William Dunlop Brackenridge

William Dunlop Brackenridge, born in Scotland in 1810, came to America in 1837.[17] His first employment was for a Philadelphia nurseryman. In 1838, he joined the United States Exploring Expedition, under Lieutenant Charles Wilkes which spent four years exploring the Pacific rim, including the Oregon country. Brackenridge collected 40,000 specimens which represented 10,000 species of plants, about 100 native living plants, and many seeds. The collection became the nucleus for the National Herbarium. Brackenridge's journal formed the basis for a report on the ferns collected by the Expedition, being published as part of the official report in 1846. His journal of occurrences while on Puget Sound was published by the Washington Historical Quarterly, under the title *Our First Official Horticulturist* (WHQ 21, pp. 218-229, 298-305; 22, pp. 42-58, 129-145, 216-270).

At nineteen, Brackenridge had been head gardener at the Edinburgh Botanical Gardens, then headed a department at the British Gardens. He emigrated to Philadelphia just a year before the Wilkes Expedition sailed. His employer there, the famed nurseryman Robert Buist, recommended him to Wilkes as a well-trained scientific observer and potentially fine collector. Time and events proved him correct.

While based at Fort Nisqually where he had set up an observatory, Lt. Wilkes ordered Brackenridge to join a party which was to cross the Cascades north of Mount Rainier and then to proceed eastward to Fort Colville, then south to the Hudson's Bay Company's Fort Walla Walla, returning along the Yakima river and back across the mountains. Brackenridge's journal gives a good account of the entire trip.[18] His conclusions were interesting. First: "A Sailor on shore is as a fish out of Water." Second: Concerning the potential value of the country visited and the contrasting views of earlier writers, he wrote, "It appears to me, that we certainly must have viewed it in a very different light from the Majority of Writers that have come out so boldly in its favor." He didn't believe that two acres out of a hundred to be found north of Walla Walla would be made to pay.

Probably the rattlesnakes and mosquitos in the Yakima canyon, confrontations with hostile Indians who tried to steal one of the horses, shortages of provisions relieved only by friendlier Indians who showed them how to dry salmon and to make camas cakes, all helped Brackenridge arrive at the unfavorable estimate of the new country. But he was impressed by some of the natural history he observed, saying about the climb through the forests that the trunks "were so straight and clean that it was seldom you could find a branch closer than 150 feet to the ground."

Another assignment led to joining a survey party to explore Gray's Harbor at the mouth of the Chehalis River. They ran into terrible weather, rain, fog, and wind gales, and found that the "harbor" was mostly mud flats. Here, too, they ran short of provisions and had to subsist on clams, berries, and dead fish carried in by the surf. They finished the survey in twenty-four days, and started back, leaving, as Lieutenant Eld put it, "this miserable hole."[19]

Brackenridge also got to visit San Francisco Bay. The trip was filled with dangers and experiences. At one time they met Captain John Sutter who was unimpressed when James Dana, a member of the party, told him that he had seen strong signs of gold in the vicinity of Mount Shasta. Later, Sutter's finding of gold in his own millrace would lead to the world's greatest gold-rush.

Brackenridge made the entire voyage with the Wilkes Expedition, and, upon returning to Washington, D.C. was permitted to build a greenhouse where the plants collected would be nurtured under the sponsorship of the new Smithsonian museum.

News of the return of the Exploring Expedition and its glamorous collections of plants, specimens and artifacts stirred great public interest. Brackenridge had to fight off those people, some in high public places, who wanted little "samples" from his collection. In fact, one of those he refused was Mrs. Tyler, the wife of the President, who tried "to pull rank" on him. Brackenridge stuck to his guns and, when Mrs. Tyler complained to the Commissioner of Patents about him, she was told that the matter was out of his hands.[20] Enough politicians and their wives were offended by Brackenridge's refusal to decimate his tender charges that an attempt was made to cut off appropriations for the project in Congress -- fortunately to no avail.

In 1855 Brackenridge bought an orchard near Baltimore and went into business as a landscape gardener and nurseryman. He also edited the horticultural department magazine, the *American Farmer*. There he lived contentedly with his wife, the former Isabella Bell, also from Scotland. They had one son. Death found him among his flowers and specimens in his 83rd year.

Archibald Menzies

David Douglas

William Fraser Tolmie

Chapter Twelve

Scottish gold

Tacoma — 1880.

It takes capital to develop a civilization from a frontier area. The American west offered many opportunities for investment to European interests during the nineteenth century. The land west of the Mississippi River generally was undeveloped, and with the presence of great natural resources in the western states and territories, foreign capital was needed and encouraged. There was also the lure of higher interest rates than could be found in Europe.

The Pacific Northwest was virgin territory, and Scottish investors were quick to realize it. Some of the key people who stepped in came on to the Pacific Northwest to survey the opportunities. Others remained in Scotland, supplying the capital and supporting these enterprises. By 1879, four major investment companies were chartered in Scotland for the sole purpose of investing money in the United States. They were the Scottish-American Investment Company, the Scottish-American Mortgage Company, the American Mortgage Company of Scotland, and the Edinburgh American Land Company. All were limited companies.[1]

These companies were based in Edinburgh, but another influential group from Dundee established the trust companies which probably had the most direct impact upon the Pacific Northwest. Dundee was home for a number of manufacturers of jute products which had a world market. The United States had been a leading customer during the Civil War since the jute was required for sandbags in the entrenchments. In the 1860's such large fortunes were made by Dundee jute merchants that they bore the laughing appellation of "the juteocracy of Scotland."

Looking toward the American west for investment outlets, one Dundee group organized the Scottish American Investment Trust. The earliest American investments made by the group were in railroad stocks and bonds. During the American Panic of 1873, when the market fell, wiping out many American companies, the Dundee company paid all due interest coupons on the company bonds to its investors. Encouraged by their example, a second group of Dundee capitalists organized the Oregon and Washington Trust Investment Company in 1873, at the very peak of the "American Panic." But this time, the field for investments would be in land mortgages.[2]

The man who promoted the organization was William Reid, at the time the vice-consul for the United States in Dundee. When Reid returned to Oregon to survey investment opportunities, his aggressive promotion techniques soon won him the awed recognition of northwestern business men who began to call him "Dundee" Reid. His keen business sense told him that, since Oregon and Washington were still frontier territory, the need for developmental capital would continue for some time to assure high interest rates.

After a short inspection tour in Oregon in 1874, Reid was appointed general manager in charge of all American operations for the new company. Using Portland as a base, he went to work to secure loans. He advertised in local newspapers and beat the drums in public places to spur the demand. One typical advertisement said: "Money to loan by the Oregon & Washington Trust Investment Company to Farmers and Landowners of Oregon and Washington Territory! Do you want to borrow Money? either — to Buy more Land for yourselves or your Sons? To Build new Houses or Barns or to Fence? To clear off Brush Land, underdrain or other wise improve your Farms? To change your present Mortgage and get a new one to be repaid each Fall from the profits of your Farm by yearly instalments payments, so as to give you three to ten years to pay up your Mortgage easily? OR ANY OTHER PURPOSE? IF YOU DO, WRITE WILLIAM REID, PORTLAND."[3]

The usual interest rates paid by borrowers was 12%. Stockholders received the first annual dividend of 6%, but the following year it was raised to 7.7%. Soon swollen with success, Reid asked the board of directors of the company for an increase in salary. The board refused. So he decided to form a savings bank, running it himself but retaining his connection with the company. Displaying no hard feelings, the company helped to finance construction and to provide capital. Two-fifths of the money needed was raised in the Pacific Northwest and the rest came from Dundee. There would also be two boards of directors — one in Portland, the other in Dundee.

A building housing both the bank and offices for the investment company was erected on First Street, in Portland. The facade of the new building was grand, something new for the frontier northwest. Adorned by several classical portraits, one of which was supposed to be a likeness of the Earl of Airlie, it honored Scot tradition and the first chairman of the Oregon and Washington Trust Investment Company back in Dundee. The artist who laid out the design gave the chairman a rather startling resemblance to Sir Francis Drake! Since Drake may have been the first European to sight the Oregon coast, the conception may have been appropriate, though the proof of that was debated then as it is today.[4] However, whether Drake sighted Oregon or never got further north than San Francisco Bay, the new bank was in business.

The new Savings Bank invested substantial funds in Portland's downtown business district. But when Reid asked for help from the investment company for the purpose of funding the developing outlying areas, the directors turned him down. This decision, plus the increasing aggressiveness and expansionist policies which Reid pursued led to more friction between the Scot promoter and the board of directors back in Dundee. Thinking to protect their interests, the board sent out Robert Connel, a Scot trained in Clydesdale in the banking business, to act as joint manager with Reid. Irate at the insult to his administrative ability, "Dundee" Reid demanded the right to sell out his interests in the company. The offer was accepted promptly. Reid was now serving as secretary of the Portland Chamber of Commerce, in addition to his other duties, and his sympathies were beginning to veer toward his fellow Oregonians.

Several other people who were important to Scottish investment in the Pacific Northwest were William Mackenzie, the secretary of the Oregon and Washington Trust Investment Company; John Paton, of New York City, whose firm served as general agent and supervisor of all regional agents for the Company in America; and the man who replaced Reid as manager in Portland, Robert Connel. Mackenzie made an inspection trip to the northwest, returning to Scotland with reports of investment opportunities as well as reports on the people working in the field. He spotted William Reid as a potential trouble-maker for the Company, particularly disliking his flamboyant methods, and so reported to his fellow directors in Scotland. John Paton, of the firm Jesup, Paton and Company, was a good example of the early public relations expert. From time to time he assured Scots investors and shareholders about the security of their investments, thus helping to stimulate a steady flow of investment capital to company coffers which, in turn, was used for American loans.

Another important role played by the Scottish investment companies was the encouragement of Scots farmers to emigrate to the American west. The largest group settled in Wisconsin and Minnesota, but a scattered number came on to the Pacific Northwest. During the 1870's the new northwest was booming. But Scotland had made earlier contributions to northwestern agriculture. The Puget Sound Agricultural Company, affiliate of the Hudson's Bay Company, sent some of its best people to the management of Company farms.[5] They also encouraged Scots to come over from the depressed agricultural areas of Scotland, a sad situation which had prevailed ever since the beginning of "the Clearances," in the Scottish Highlands, where farmers were driven out to make room for great herds of sheep.

One typical Scot who came to farm was Robert Firth. Born in the Orkney Islands, in 1830, Firth entered the service of the Hudson's Bay Company when just nineteen years of age. He landed first in Victoria in 1849, after a six month trip from England via Cape Horn. For several years he was employed there by the Company. Then, in 1862 he was trans-

ferred to the San Juan islands, and placed in charge of Company holdings. Here he raised sheep and cattle, supplying Victoria and Company
outposts. After San Juan island was awarded to the United States the
Company turned over the land to Firth, who homesteaded there and became an American citizen. Following the withdrawal of American troops
who had been stationed on San Juan during the comic opera "Pig War,"
Firth occupied the house which had been built on San Juan for Captain
George Pickett. This was the same Pickett who later launched the famous
charge of the Confederacy at Gettysburg. The Firth acres became known
as Bellevue Farm, and he remained there until his death in 1903. He left
the farm to his daughter who eventually sold it to another Scot, a Mr.
McRae.[6]

The boom times of the 1870's also saw the expansion of other key
northwest industries which were aided by the infusion of Scottish capital.
Canneries on the Columbia River were grossing more than three million
a year by the end of the decade. Wheat ranches were now selling 176,000
tons of wheat annually to Great Britain alone. Railroad production was ex-
panding, keeping pace with the need for shipping agricultural products.
As for the maritime industry, Scottish interests had been involved for
decades. The ports of the northwest were long familiar to Scot shipping,
many of the ships not only having been built at Glasgow, but were also
run by Scots — captains, other officers, and ships' engineers who had received their training "Clydeside." Scottish capital was invested in just
about every phase of northwest development.

The best account of the Scottish role in the development of the American west is an excellent pioneer study by W. Turrentine Jackson, *The
Enterprising Scot.* Published originally in Edinburgh, the book is now
available from an American publisher. To that author I am indebted for
many of the facts in this chapter. Professor Jackson pointed the way for
many future studies, the subject of Scottish investment in America being
so broad. Much can still be done, in terms of "smoking out" the records
which still exist in Scotland and in business archives in the United States,
particularly where American companies and Scottish companies had joint
interests.[7]

Another interesting project for the student would be to locate surviv-
ing newspaper and promotional brochures, by means of which the word
was spread to farmers or would-be borrowers. Recently, in Victoria, I
found several issues of *The Orkney and Shetland American,* an ethnic
newspaper published in the 1880's and 1890's in Chicago.[8] The subscrip-
tion list came from Scots all over America. One of the most interesting articles was a report from Portland. The advertisements were classic.

When in London a few years ago, I visited Glyn, Mills & Company, an old bank with historic American connections. For one thing they had been a depository for the Hudson's Bay Company since about 1820. Their archives included files on the story of American and Canadian railroad development, the Canadian Pacific and the Great Northern, in particular, which they helped to finance.[9] The bank's Scottish involvement was also interesting. A number of these British banks have archives which hold the records of predecessor banks or corporations, and Glyn, Mills and Company was no exception.

It is a fascinating paradox that at a time when absentee landlords were raising rents or driving farmers from the land to make room for sheep, to the south of them, in Edinburgh and Dundee, Scottish investment companies were inviting the Scot farmer to emigrate to America.[10] The connection, if any, needs to be spelled out, and would make a good subject for someone's thesis.

The title of this chapter, *Scottish Gold*, may have led the reader to think it dealt with mining rather than investment. Scottish capital *was* invested in western mining, and W. Turrentine Jackson's book explores that subject, too. But most of the mining took place out of the northwest, at least where Scottish capital was involved. When the Klondyke gold rush exploded, in 1898, Scots were present and aware of investment possibilities, but the setting was Canada's Yukon Territory, and that area is geographically remote from the region covered by this book.[11]

Another interesting fact was cited by Gordon Donaldson in his book *The Scot Overseas* (page 123) which concerns Scottish influence upon western ranching and cattle breeding. He noted that three-quarters of the foreign investment in the United States during the late 1870's and the 1880's, in ranching alone, came from Scotland. During that period the famed Aberdeen-Angus strain was introduced, a fact which rejoices our contemporary Washingtonian, Stuart Anderson, of Scottish descent, rancher and *restauranteur extraordinaire*. Much remains to be done in a study of northwestern ranching, whereas the southwest, particularly Texas, has been covered by studies.

Epilogue

In a book of this length some things are left out by necessity. Other things receive an emphasis which may not please a demanding reader. By using folklore as well as history it was my purpose to include background material which would help us to understand the Scottish heritage, particularly in how it differs from other ethnic traditions. In other words, how did the northwestern citizen of Scot descent get that way? To me there seems no other way in which to give a well-rounded characterization of a distinctive people.

Several things could have been added to the chapters on customs and entertainments. Golfers will shrink in horror to learn that there is nothing at all on the Scottish invention of this popular sport. For those who feel cheated by this, there is plentiful literature available for further study of the history of golf, St. Andrew's, of Alexander Baillie, founder of the second golf club on the Pacific Coast (at Tacoma), etc. Nor is there anything on the sport of curling, a distinctive Scottish pastime. And where is the chapter on Scotch whiskey? Alas, not here.

What concerns me is the paucity of material at hand concerning the Scottish woman. There is much room for further study of the great contributions she made to northwest history. Abigail Scott Duniway could have occupied a key section of the chapter on women. Fortunately, there is a new biography of this great woman which will be published soon. But there must be many more, mute and glorious, whose stories need telling.

It would have been fun to include a generous sampling of the folk songs and ballads of the Scot with particular attention to the profound ways in which folklore changes in a new environment. First comes the immigrant, bringing the folklore which was his Old World heritage; then we see the folklore subjected to the environments of the New World, and later to the influence of American popular lore, and tradition in the literary sense, with the result that the ethnic materials from his former homeland are modified or supplanted. At the same time, indigenous regional and occupational lores are emerging, such as the songs and legends of the logger or the sailor. This is a continuous process, from the very beginning of emigration to America in 1607. These ideas are a paraphrase of those expressed by Tristram Coffin and Hennig Cohen, in *Folklore in America*, especially in their introduction. (Anchor Books, 1970.)

The crucial process of *transition* is treated in one chapter through the use of only a few samples of the Scot-American experience. The technique could be used for any ethnic group, and perhaps with more success, particularly if the subject was explored in depth, in terms of acculturation and absorption. Here is a tremendously rich field for investigation by the student of ethnic history.

Finally, I regret that time did not permit a concentration on some of the people less famous than, say, Dr. McLoughlin. His story is so well known that little could be added, except as exemplary of an outstanding, even heroic contribution. One who deserved fuller treatment was James Christie, one of the last northwest explorers. There are many others. Last of all, though the time spent upon research, interviews, and documentation for this book was unbelievably great, they all provided much enjoyment. A Scottish *envoi* seems in order:

> "Fairweill thairfoir my hairt adew
> fairweill and have gudnicht.
> God graunt that we doe never rew
> bot to have chosen richt."

Footnotes

Introduction

1. Boswell, James: *Life of Samuel Johnson,* Vol I, page 264.
2. Boswell, James: *A Tour to the Hebrides,* New York, 1936. The first publication of the unexpurgated manuscript. Page 5.
3. Ibid.
4. Op. cit.
5. Ibid.
6. The songs are not reproduced in this edition.
7. Beaglehole, J. C. *The Life of Captain James Cook,* Stanford, 1974, pages 451-452; Beaglehole, J. C. *Bibliography of Captain James Cook,* Sydney, Australia, 1970, page 618.
8. Beaglehole, J. C. *Bibliography of Captain James Cook,* op. cit.
9. Tocqueville, Alexis de: *Democracy in America,* ed. by Phillips Bradley, New York, 1945.
10. *Encyclopedia Britannica:* Vol. 20, Chicago, 1966. Pages 138-170.
11. Erickson, Charlotte: *The Invisible Immigrants,* op. cit.
12. *Scottish Heritage,* Edinburgh, n. d. *The World's Debt to Scotland,* pages 31-35.
13. Dorson, Richard: *American Folklore and the Historian,* Chicago, 1971, Page 35.
14. Ibid.
15. Barrie, Sir James: *What Every Woman Knows,* a comedy. Page 223, Act II (in *Representative Plays,* New York, 1926).
16. Black, G. F.: *Scotland's Mark on America,* New York, 1921. Page 40.
17. Ibid.
18. *The American Archivist,* July, 1976. Pages 319-328.
19. Ibid.
20. *The Beaver* has carried many important articles on the Scot in fur trade history. A list of the *Hudson's Bay Record Society* publications, available from HBC, in Winnipeg, Canada, also has a number of the most important journals in print i.e. *McLoughlin's Correspondence,* and the *Hudson's Bay Miscellany,* 1670-1870, (1975). Simpson's *Character Book* of 1832, in which he makes frequently acidulous appraisals of the men under his command, is included, together with a list of Chief Factors and Chief Traders, and an introduction by the editor, Glyndwr Williams, which was helped by comments from John S. Galbraith and Sylvia Van Kirk. The importance of the "Character Book," with Simpson's secret commentaries on various influential HBC people cannot be over-estimated. One must remember, however, that he sometimes changed his ideas later, or was more charitable, and that the comments in the *"Character Book"* were intended for himself alone. The Arthur Clark *Mountain Men and Fur-Traders* series is also useful. (Glendale, California)

Prologue

1. In *Astoria* Washington Irving expressed mixed sentiments about the Scots in the fur trade. Sometimes he characterized them as "lords of the streams and forests," at other times as "Nabobs" who depended upon a flock of retainers who did their bidding in a manner akin to the caste requirements back in Scotland.
2. Dorson, Richard: *American Folklore and the Historian,* Chicago, 1971. Page 189.
3. Bryce, George: *The Scotsman in Canada,* Toronto, 1911. Introduction.

4. The *Center for Northwest Folklore*, a department of the Washington State Historical Society, was organized only recently. Despite that, its collections already contain a good beginning in ethnic history: manuscripts, books, pictures, and artifacts.

5. *The Scots Magazine*, January 1971, *Waters of Change*, pages 322, 330.

6. Erickson, Charlotte: *The Invisible Immigrants*, Coral Gables, Fla., 1972.

7. Notestein, Wallace: *The Scot in History*, Westport, Conn., 1970. (Reprint of Yale ed., 1946.)

8. The Edinburgh cab driver was correct, as reference to the *Encyclopedia Britannica* would confirm. That day, the Queen was coming to town, to stay at Holyrood Castle, a fact which the driver attributed to her recognition of Scottish leadership!

9. *A Short History of the Hudson's Bay Company*, Tacoma, 1970, edited in a new edition by Bruce Le Roy, with introduction and trip itinerary. Illustrated from the collections in the Washington State Historical Society. (Privately printed and not for sale.)

10. Crick, Bernard: *A Guide to Manuscripts Relating to America in Great Britain and Ireland*, Oxford University Press, 1961.

11. Percy, Bishop: *Reliques of Ancient British Poetry*, London, 1765. The extract is from *Scotish Fields*, a ballad about a battle between the English and the Scots, one of many such, in Anglo-Scottish history.

12. Beaglehole, J. C. *The Life of Captain James Cook*, Stanford, 1974, pages 2-3.

13. Garraty, John: *Encyclopedia of American Biography*, New York, 1974.

14. *Northwest History in Art*, edited, with introduction by Bruce Le Roy, Tacoma, 1963. Pages 7, 11, 12, 13, 21. Unpaged catalogue.

Chapter One, A Journey Home

1. *Murdock Genealogy*: Goodspeed & Co. Boston, 1925, *The Murdock Family*, pages 6-9. Admiral Joseph Ballard Murdock, compiler of the 274 page book, performed considerable research in Scotland, particularly in Galloway. Admiral Murdock pointed out that the family name was taken from the Norse (Muir-dach) translated to mean "warrior of the sea." This must have been comforting to the old sea dog who served as Commander-in-chief of the U.S. Asiatic Fleet during the Chinese Revolution. He was a member of the American Philosophical Society and the Franklin Institute following his retirement in 1913.

2. Murdock, Admiral Joseph Ballard: *The Murdock Family*, page 8.

3. Family tradition has it that Robert Murdock fled Scotland just a few months before the Revolution of 1688 which placed William of Orange upon the throne of England. The first record of Robert Murdock's arrival in America is that of his marriage at Roxbury, Massachusetts Bay Colony, in 1692. There is also a deed of sale for land in Cambridge, in 1693, when he and his brother-in-law, Nathanael Stedman, disposed of part of the estate of his father-in-law. There were a number of Murdock records in Plymouth Colony (those of a brother, John Murdock), which indicate that they both arrived in America either in 1687 or 1688. Several Robert Murdock documents are in the archives of Suffolk County, in Boston, beginning in 1703.

4. McKerlie, P. H. *History of the Owners and their Lands in Galloway*, as quoted by Admiral Murdock on page 8 in the *Murdock Genealogy*. (McKerlie pub. in Edinburgh, 1870-1879.)

5. *The Murdock Family,* op. cit. pages 6-8; Sir Walter Scott: *Tales of a Grandfather,* quoted on pages 6, 7.

6. There are conflicting stories about the Coat of Arms. One is the version above; the other is that as a sept of Clan Donald, the raven was a symbol of the Norse inheritance through Somerled, King of the Scots, and his progeny who acquired the title "Macdonald of the Isles." The raven was the sacred bird of Woden, chief god of the Norse. As such, various clans and septs affiliated with Clan Donald have the raven crest.

7. *A Short History of the Hudson's Bay Company,* Tacoma, 1970. Edited, with introduction, by Bruce Le Roy. In celebrating the 300th anniversary of the Hudson's Bay Company, the delegation from the Washington State Historical Society also *made* history. The day following the celebration the Governor of the Company, Lord Amory, announced that the Company was moving its headquarters to Winnipeg. Ours, then, was the last American contingent to meet on its original grounds with the Governor and Company of Adventurers Trading Into Hudson's Bay. As noted in the *Bibliographical Essay,* all of the Company's records for the first two hundred years (1670-1870) were moved to the new "Beaver House," in Canada. This is where students of northwest history must go in future to trace the fur trade history of this area, and the people who created it.

8. Johnson, Gerald W. *The First Captain, the Story of John Paul Jones,* New York, 1947, page 48 ff.

9. Ibid. pages 178 ff.

10. The letter which John Paul Jones directed to Lady Selkirk is still at St. Mary's Isle. A facsimile of two pages is reproduced in this book. See also *John Paul Jones, Commemoration at Annapolis,* Government Printing Office, 1970. Lord Selkirk's reply is on pages 127-130, and return of the silver is acknowledged on pages 131-132. This book is still in print at GPO.

11. Selkirk, Thomas Douglas, Fifth Earl of: *Observations on the Present State of the Highlands of Scotland, With a View of the Causes and Probable Consequences of Emigration,* London 1805. Lord Selkirk argues in favor of emigration from Scotland. Also includes an account of the first colony he established for Scottish emigrants at Prince Edward Island in 1803. See also: Selkirk: *A Sketch of the British Fur Trade in North America; with Observations Relative to the North-West Company of Montreal.* Relates to the Red River settlement, and also to the bitter feud between the North West Company and the Hudson's Bay Company.

12. *The Beaver,* Winter 1966. pp. 44-51. Marwick, Ernest W.: *Chief Factor James Sutherland and his Orkney Correspondence.* Letters back to his family in Scotland from Sutherland, who was in charge of the Red River settlement at the time a large party was sent down to Puget Sound and the Willamette Valley.

13. *The Beaver,* Spring 1971. Betts, William J.: *From Red River to the Columbia, the Story of a Migration.* Pages 50-55. William Fraser Tolmie recorded in his journal that he met the party at Fort Garry as they started south for Puget Sound. Tolmie was Factor at Fort Nisqually and would become a helpful neighbor to his fellow Scots.

14. Porter, Mae Reed, and Davenport, Odessa: *Scotsman in Buckskin, Sir William Drummond Stewart and the Rocky Mountain Fur Trade,* New York, 1963.

15. De Voto, Bernard: *Across the Wide Missouri,* Boston, 1947.

16. *Lewis and Clark's America: A Voyage of Discovery.* Seattle Art Museum, 1976.

Catalogue of this exhibit of art and photography contains reproductions of ten Miller paintings and sketches.

17. Copies of Stewart-Sublette letters in the Washington State Historical Society Library.

Chapter Two, From the Heather to the Sea

1. Beaglehole, J. C. *The Life of Captain James Cook,* Stanford, 1974, pages 2-3.
2. *Passport to Glory: Benjamin Franklin and Captain Cook,* Tacoma, 1975. The letter is reproduced in facsimile with a "translation" and an introduction by Bruce Le Roy. A. Bicentennial publication.
3. Beaglehole, J. C. *The Life of Captain James Cook,* op. cit. pages 665-672.
4. *The Northwest Coast.* Edward Eberstadt, Number 119, New York 1941, pages 70-71. Other accounts exist, but I like the insertion, that the Captain muttered, as he fell to the deck mortally wounded by the passing ship's salute, "Damme, too much English on the ball!" This catalogue is an excellent reference for early northwest explorations literature.
5. Manuscript collections, Washington State Historical Society. Copies of the letters and memorials sent to Congress by the Kendrick family.
6. The Hawaii State Archives and the Hawaii Historical Society have contemporary accounts of Douglas' death. One speculates that the circumstances of death pointed to murder, rather than to an accident, a highly doubtful theory, though possible.
7. *The Life and Adventures of John Nicol, Mariner,* Edinburgh, 1822. Reprinted, with introduction by Gordon Grant, by Farrar & Rinehart, New York, 1936.
8. Ibid. Pages 81 ff. (1936 edition)
9. La Perouse, Jean Francois Galaup: *A Voyage Round the World in the Years 1785-88,* London, 1797.
10. Strange, James: *Journal and Narrative of the Commercial Expedition from Bombay to the North-West Coast of America,* Madras, 1928.
11. Meares, John: *Voyages Made in the Years 1788-89, from China to the Northwest Coast of America. To which are prefixed the Narrative of a Voyage performed in 1786, from Bengal, in the Ship "Nootka;" Observations on the Probable Existence of a Northwest Passage; and some account of the Trade Between the Northwest Coast and China.* London, 1790.
12. *Official Papers relative to the Dispute between the Courts of Great Britain and Spain, on the Subject of the Ships Captured in Nootka Sound, and the Negotiation that followed thereon; together with the Proceedings of both Houses of Parliament on the King's Message: to which are added the Report of M. de Mirabeau, etc.* London, 1790.
13. *The Life and Adventures of John Nicol, Mariner.* Op. Cit. Page 187.
14. Southworth, John Van Duyn: *The Ancient Fleets.* New York, 1968. Pages 268, 277-278, 280-281; also Moncreiffe & Hicks: *The Highland Clans,* London, 1967. Introduction *The Highlands,* pages 10-41.
15. Lewis and Dryden *Marine History of the Pacific Northwest,* Portland, 1895. Traces Clyde-built ships to Pacific Northwest.
16. Ibid.
17. Ibid.
18. *The Beaver,* June 1953. *He Piloted the Beaver,* by Donald H. Clark. Pages 46-47.
19. *Nonsuch, Hudson's Bay Company ship replica.* London, 1969, Introduction by the

Rt. Hon. Viscount Amory, Governor, Hudson's Bay Company; text by Basil Greenhill.

20. Ibid.
21. *A Short History of the Hudson's Bay Company.* Tacoma, 1970. See "Itinerary," at the end of the book.
22. *The Times,* London, May 2nd, 1970.

Chapter Three, White-Headed Eagle

1. Hussey, John A. *The History of Fort Vancouver and its Physical Structure.* Tacoma, 1958. Pages 1-2.
2. McArthur, Lewis A. *Oregon Geographic Names.* Portland, 1952. Page 426.
3. Drury, Clifford M. *Marcus and Narcissa Whitman and the Opening of Old Oregon.* Glendale, 1973. Pages 213-217; Narcissa Whitman's original journal is in the collections of the Washington State Historical Society, so identified by Dr. Drury. See footnote on page 199 (Drury).
4. Ibid. Page 213.
5. Cogswell, Philip, Jr. *Capitol Names.* Portland, 1977. Pages 79-81.
6. Ibid.
7. Lamb, W. Kaye; *John McLoughlin,* in the Introduction to *McLoughlin's Fort Vancouver Letters,* 1844-46, Toronto, 1944. Pages LXII-III.

Chapter Four, Transition

1. Tolmie, William Fraser: *Physician and Fur Trader: The Journal of William Fraser Tolmie,* Portland, 1956.
2. Tolmie, William Fraser: letters to Thomas Chambers, *The Chambers Collection,* edited by Frank Green, Washington State Historical Society, Tacoma, 1972.
3. Tolmie, op. cit., edited, with notes by his son, Simon Fraser Tolmie, Vancouver, 1963.
4. McKinlay, Archibald: McKinlay Papers, Washington State Historical Society. From McKinlay's letter book, 1884.
5. Sampson, William: *John McLoughlin's Business Correspondence,* 1847-1848. Seattle, 1971. Pages 74-76.
6. Ibid.
7. Edward Huggins papers, Washington State Historical Society. The Huntington Library and Yale University have complementary collections of Huggins' letters.
8. *Tacoma Ledger,* May 22, 1892.
9. *Pioneer Reminiscences of Puget Sound, or the Tragedy of Leschi,* Ezra Meeker. Seattle, 1905.

Chapter Five, Scottish Folk Customs

1. Dorson, Richard: *American Folklore and the Historian.* Chicago, op. cit. page 197; also see Dorson, Richard: *American Folklore.* Chicago, 1959. Chapters on *Regional Folk Cultures* (pages 74-134) and *Immigrant Folklore* (pages 135-165).
2. *The Scottish Tradition in Canada.* Toronto, 1976. See the chapter *Scottish Place-Names in Canada,* by Watson Kirkconnell, pages 311-321.
3. Meany, Edmond: *Origin of Washington Geographic Names.* Seattle 1923; also Hitchman, Robert: *Name-Calling: Notes on the Discovery and Exploration of the Olympic Peninsula,* Seattle, *The Mountaineer,* 1959. (Separate reprint.)
4. Ibid. (Meany). Also should be mentioned Mount McLoughlin, in Jackson County, Oregon, named in honor of Dr. John McLoughlin, recognized by the U.S. Board

of Geographic Names in 1912. For the interesting background of this action see *Oregon Geographic Names,* by McArthur, op. cit. pages 425-426.

5. Ibid. (McArthur, OGN.)
6. Cockburn, Henry: *Journals,* 2 vol. Edinburgh, 1874; *Memorials of his Time,* ed. by Karl Miller, Chicago, 1974; pages 388-390.
7. *The Cronies Club.* Tacoma, 1896. No author credited. Privately printed.
8. Ibid.
9. I have been unable to locate any comparable organization still extant, excluding the larger, more formal, Caledonian and St. Andrews Societies. The charm of The Cronies Club lay in its small size, intimacy, and the fact that most of the members either emigrated to the Pacific Northwest or were, at most, second generation.

Chapter Six, Traditional Observances

1. *The Scots Book*: Edited by Ronald Macdonald Douglas. London, 1935. This is one of those little books which travelers to Scotland found useful between the two World Wars. It is chock-full of facts, ballads, legends, some history (untrustworthy, depending upon who compiled it) and lots of fun. Another such book, more accessible, is *The Scots Weekend,* by Donald and Catherine Carswell, London, 1936. Both are excellent if one tempers acceptance with critical judgment.
2. *The Caledonian Society Newsletter*: *January* 1975: "Burns Dinner," and the newsletter for January 1976, *The Haggis is a Wondrous Beast.* Published in Honolulu.
3. Ibid. January 1976. The poet who added to the *Selkirk Grace* was Mr. R. R. Walker, of Scone, Scotland.
4. *The Caledonian Society Newsletter, November,* 1975. The "Betwixt and Between Party" was held on December 27th. Scots from all over Canada and the northwestern United States attended.
5. *The Royal Hudson Tour.* The Ministry of the Provincial Secretary and Travel Industry, Victoria, B.C. 1977. See "Land of Festival." Seattle and Tacoma newspapers, in Washington, and Portland and Salem newspapers, in Oregon, always announce the Highland Games and the events are covered by television. In Canada, the "Games" are a national pastime.
6. *The Caledonian Newsletter, September,* 1975. Inger McClennan represented the Society at the "Gathering" in Scotland.
7. *Guinness Book of Records,* London, 1974. Also the Caledonian Society Newsletter, April, 1975.
8 *The Caledonian Newsletter, February* 1976. Quote: "In Salute to the Year of the Dragon the Society will dedicate a party an evening to the mystery of Scotland's favorite creature, the Loch Ness Monster . . . scaly and firebreathing party games, country, old-time and serpentine dancing."

Chapter Seven, Scottish Proverbs

1. *Scottish Proverbs*: James Kelly. Edinburgh, 1718. The book went through many printings. There may have been earlier editions, according to a publisher's note.
2. Ibid. Introduction.
3. Ibid. For comparison with American folk expressions of ethnic origin, see *American Folklore,* edited by Tristram Coffin, III, in the *Voice of America Forum Lectures,* distributed by the U.S. Information Agency. The relevant chapter is "The

Wisdom of Many," on "Proverbs and Proverbial Expressions," by Ray B. Browne, pages 217-230.

4. All of these proverbial sayings were taken from *Scottish Proverbs*, op. cit. and discussed with northwestern Scottish emigrants or descendants for reactions and comments.

5. Tracking down proverbial expressions by ethnic usage is one of the most neglected techniques and one of the potentially most rewarding. Only professional folklorists and a few dedicated amateurs are using the method, and, generally, are not concerned about applying their findings to ethnic history. Here is a wide-open field for students of regional or ethnic history, linking historical methodology with the techniques of the field-worker in folklore.

Chapter Eight, Things that go Bump in the Night

1. *More Highland Folktales*, edited by R. Macdonald Robertson, Edinburgh, 1964. See chapter on *Witchcraft*, pages 61-84; also *Highways and Byways in Galloway & Carrick*: Thomson, Hugh, London, 1919, page 480-484. Many books and monographs on Scottish witchcraft are available, see bibliographies.

2. *The Poetical Works of Robert Burns*, in three volumes. London, 1823. Burns' poetry was published in hundreds of different editions and formats. His use of Scottish folklore was all-pervasive in his poetry. Beginning with the famous "Tam O'Shanter," other poems, such as *Halloween*, with his footnotes, are distillations of folk belief and practice i.e. ". . . a night when witches, devils, and other mischief-making beings are all abroad on their baneful, midnight errands." His notes on the peculiar Scottish ceremonies on Halloween are fabulous, with recipes for certain charms which must be invoked.

3. Scott, Sir Walter: *Letters on Demonology and Witchcraft*, London, 1831. Scott met Burns when he visited Edinburgh in the winter of 1786-1787, when Scott was only 15 years old. The two shared an intense interest in Scottish folklore. Scott's travels and interviews throughout Scotland provided a wealth of information for his books, as well as a host of correspondents on such subjects as early witchcraft practices.

4. *Seattle Post-Intelligencer*: Oct. 31, 1976, page C-1; April 26, 1977, page C-1.

5. *More Highland Folk Tales*, op. cit. page 64.

6. TO THE WORLD!!! A broadside, published by James W. Nesmith, Oregon City, June 7, 1847. Republished in *Oregon Imprints*, 1847-1870, by Douglas C. McMurtrie; introduction by Albert H. Allen, University of Oregon Publications, Eugene, Oregon.

7. *More Highland Folk Tales*, op. cit. "*Curing the Murrain*" pages 79-80.

8. *The Scots Book*, op. cit. "*Second Sight*,' pages 130-133.

9. Elton Cormier, on the staff of the Washington State Historical Society, originally from Louisiana, is a walking encyclopedia of native folklore, especially of the Creole tradition.

10. There is a variation on this famous invocation, in Scottish dialect: "Frae Witches, Warlocks, an' Wurricoes, an' Evil Spirits, an' a' Things that gang Bump i' the nicht, Guid Lord, deliver us!"

Chapter Nine, Ballads and Folk Songs

1. *Bartlett's Familiar Quotations*, Boston, 1955, page 650 b. Quoted from Scott, Sir Walter, *The Monastery*, 1825, Chapter 25, *The Border Ballad*, and from William Dunbar, Scottish poet (c. 1460-c. 1520).

2. Child, Francis. *The English and Scottish Popular Ballads*, 5 vols. Boston, 1882-1898. See Professor Child's Introduction. Also see Sharp, Cecil J. *English Folk Songs from the Southern Appalachians*, 2 vols. London, 1932. Scottish songs are included.

3. Child, op. cit.

4. Blankenship, Russell: *And There Were Men*, New York, 1942, pages 13, 25; *Told by the Pioneers*, 3 vols. Olympia, 1938. These oral interviews were gathered as a WPA project. Their ethnic and geographical spread make a fertile source-book. The WPA guidebooks for the northwestern states are also valuable. Demographic studies conducted by the various states generally lump Scots, Welsh, Irish, and English under one head — the British Isles.

5. Judy Collins, *Golden Apples of the Sun*, Elektra Records, *The Great Selchie of Shule Skerry.* "The seal man is an enchanted creature that normally dwells in the sea, but occasionally comes to land to pass as an ordinary man, begetting in the song a child by a normal woman. Many families in the Scottish islands trace their ancestry to sealmen, and because of a totemic taboo, will not taste seal meat." Also, Joan Baez. Vol. 2, Vanguard records, *Silkie* (Child 113). See liner notes on the origin of the ballad, one listed as 113 by Professor Child in his *The English and Scottish Popular Ballads*, op. cit.

6. If John Galt wrote the ballad it grew out of his visit to fur-trade posts in eastern Canada, but the piece has long been known in western Canada. I first saw it on a signboard in Trounce Alley, in Victoria, British Columbia. There is no consensus concerning the authorship of the ballad. *The Gallovidian*, a historical magazine published in Scotland, made a good case for Galt in its 1934 annual issue. The article is *John Galt And The Canadian Boat Song*, pages 90-92.

7. *Astoria*, op. cit.

8. *Adventurers*. A ballad by T. E. Smale, of Winnipeg, published in *The Beaver*, June 1933, page 69.

9. Percy, Bishop. *Reliques of Ancient British Poetry*, London, 1765. The ballad is taken from *The Percy Folio of Old English Ballads and Romances*, from the text provided by F. J. Furnivall and J. W. Hales, published in London, in 1905, pages 127-142.

10. MacLeod, Margaret. *Bard of the Prairies*. Both *Lord Selkirk at Fort William*, and *The Battle of Seven Oaks*, by Pierre Falcon, appear in French with an English translation in an article in *The Beaver*, Spring 1956, pages 20-26.

11. Wallace, W. Stewart. *Documents Relating to the North West Company*, Toronto, 1934. Introduction.

12. *The Scots Book*, op. cit. page 280.

13. *An Apprentice Scotty's Greeting*. A ballad by James Brodie, Fort Vermilion, published in *The Beaver*, December 1930.

14. *A Rhapsody*. A ballad by William Thomson, published in the *Orkney and Shetland American*, October 1890, page 4.

15. Hutchison, Bruce. *The Fraser*, Toronto, 1950, pages 169-170. Jamie Anderson was famed as the poet of Barkerville, mining town in the Cariboo, now restored and an historic site.

16. Ibid.

17. *The Scot and his money*, by F. S. Taylor, in *Scottish Heritage, Edinburgh*, n.d. Published by The Scottish Tourist Board. Pages 24-30. Also, bracketed in same piece, *A Scot gets his money back*, the story of George Murdoch (or Baillie Mur-

doch) who made the government in London repay the city of Glasgow for quartering troops there in 1745. He was later Lord Provost of Glasgow and his cousin, John Murdoch, was tutor to the poet Robert Burns, in 1765 and 1766, when Murdoch was just 18 years old. (Members of the Murdoch family who came to America generally spelled the name with a "k" thereafter i.e. "Murdock.")

18. These jokes I heard at different times from Scottish informants in this area. I later found them published in various places, including *The Scots Book*. As for Scottish teachers, let us pray that young John Murdoch didn't teach Master Robert Burns with the same ferocity attributed to *some* Scottish schoolmasters. The Duke of Edinburgh graduated from Gordonstoun, a Scottish school noted for its discipline and severity. So impressed was he that he sent Prince Charles and Prince Andrew to the same school. *On a Schoolmaster* tells it thus: "Mr. Rhind is very kind, he goes to kirk on Sunday; he prays to God to give him strength to skelp the bairns on Monday."

19. *The Scots Book,* op. cit.

20. Ibid. See also the introduction to Scott's *Minstrelsy of the Scottish Border* for an excellent presentation of the way in which such rebellions crept into the historical ballads.

21. Scott, Sir Walter: *Tales of a Grandfather*, Vol I, Philadelphia, n.d. (reprint of 1828 ed.).

22. *The Scots Book,* op. cit. See also *The Scots Weekend,* op. cit. for more fancy epitaphs, including one that has been lifted and adapted to western folklore. It is called *An Aberdeen Favorite,* on page 176. In the American west they merely changed the name of the town. One places the action in Butte, Montana.

23. This is now going forward, for an unpublished manuscript — a book of Northwest folk songs & ballads, in progress.

24. Ron McLean, of Winthrop, has written beautiful songs of mountains. Available on tapes from the composer.

25. Rosalie Sorrels has produced records for *Folkways,* especially of Idaho folk songs, plus other Rocky Mountain ballads.

26. His autobiographical notes in *Bound for Glory* do not give a clue.

27. *English and Scottish Popular Ballads,* Cambridge edition, Boston, 1932. Notes by George Lyman Kittredge in the introduction spell out the rules governing the classical Scots ballad. "Impersonality" is highly important.

28. Woody Guthrie considered himself a spokesman for the laborer, the migrant worker, and the union organizer. When World War II came along he painted a slogan on his guitar — "this machine kills fascists." Words were always potential weapons, to Woody.

29. Personal observation. For a good example of the beginning process, listen to a classroom of second-graders singing one of Guthrie's more well-known songs. "From Manhattan to the Golden Gate" will have a new "geography," akin to one child who marched around during an ethnic Christmas program, singing something different from his classmates. When his teacher got near, instead of "O Tannenbaum," she heard the child singing "O atom bomb!" Peace on earth, good will to men!

30. *Minstrelsy of the Scottish Border,* op. cit. Pages 337-338.

31. Ibid. Scott lists both variants in Part II, "Romantic Ballads."

32. Rydberg, V.: *Teutonic Mythology* (English translation) 1889, London. See *Woden, Chief of the Gods.*

33. *Tales of the Covenanters*, Kilmarnock, Scotland, n.d. page 264.
34. *Minstrelsy of the Scottish Border*, op. cit. pages 275-276.
35. Ibid. Page 278.
36. Reprinting of this rare book would be a great service to folklorists. If the author has been identified I have not been able to find the reference. His pseudonym indicates he may have been an Anglican clergyman.
37. "Mixed" in the sense that someone of the Dominie's persuasion might be offended. "Thou'rt made an officer to Satan" is a terrible way to refer to a Presbyterian minister of the gospel. That is one of the milder condemnations which "Jacob Curate" employed.
38. The other two are *Retreat of the Ten Thousand*, a ballad about an aborted filibustering raid by American sailors in China in 1854 which was blamed on Robert McLane, the U.S. Commissioner. The story is told in the *China Journal of Edward Le Roy*: 1853-1854. Le Roy was McLane's secretary. The other ballad is *Christine Le Roy*, about a fatal charmer in western folklore whom I have adopted into the family, not being able to prove the connection.
39. The ballad is reproduced in *Rocky Mountain Ballads*, by Austin and Alta Fife, who say that it is still sung at pioneer picnics.
40. *The Scottish Song Book*, no place, no date. *The Scottish Emigrant's Farewell* appears to be an Edinburgh publication of the early 19th century, based upon comparisons with similar books.

Chapter Ten, The Women: liberated and otherwise

1. I hasten to mention that this is not a *complete* list. A number of the women writers cited in this book have made and are making great contributions to historical literature. An expanded list would include Grace Lee Nute, Margaret Arnett MacLeod, Iris Allan, Margaret Mead, citing only those who have written for *The Beaver*. Several are of Scottish descent.
2. Lamb, W. Kaye: *The Mystery of Mrs. Barkley's Diary*, published in *British Columbia Historical Quarterly*, Vol. VI, Number 1.
3. Holbrook, Stewart: *The Columbia*, New York, 1956.
4. Ibid.
5. *Women and the Fur Trade, The Beaver*, Winter, 1972. A discerning article by Sylvia Van Kirk, who analyzed the tensions which grew between the Indian or mixed blood wives of the traders, and the women who came from Scotland to join or to marry fur-traders.
6. *Ranald Macdonald, Adventurer*, by Ralph P. Edgerton, *The Pacific Northwesterner*, Winter 1969, Vol. 13, Number 1.
7. *Journey for Frances*, edited with introduction by Grace Lee Nute; *The Beaver*, December, 1953; March, 1954; Summer, 1954.
8. *A Pioneer Gentlewoman in British Columbia: The Recollections of Susan Allison* edited by Margaret A. Ormsby; Vancouver, B.C. 1976.
9. Thompson, David: *Narrative of Explorations in Western America*, 1714-1812. Champlain Society, Toronto, 1916. Thompson was part Welsh.
10. *Murdock Family History*, op. cit.

Chapter Eleven, Botanizing Scots

1. *Menzies' Journal of Vancouver's Voyage, April to October,* 1792, edited by Charles Francis Newcombe and John Forsyth; Victoria, 1923.
2. Ibid. A copy of the original journal, which is in the British Museum, is in the Archives of British Columbia on microfilm.
3. Douglas, David. *Journal Kept by David Douglas during his Travels in North America,* 1823-1827, London, 1914.
4. *Encyclopedia Britannica,* Vol. 7, page 608, 1966 Edition.
5. *Journal,* op. cit.
6. *Hudson's Bay Miscellany,* 1670-1870, edited with introductions by Glyndwr Williams, Winnipeg, 1975. Hargraves' appraisal differed radically from that of Sir George Simpson, who at first characterized McKenzie, in unflattering terms, as "a large, heavy, inactive, indolent Man, who makes a very bad use of the Talents he possesses . . ." Simpson changed his opinion later, writing a good letter about McKenzie to the HBC London Committee. See pages 179-180 for comparison, and footnote on Simpson's change of heart on page 179, footnote 4.
7. Bancroft, H. H.: *History of British Columbia,* Vol. 32, page 135; also see Holbrook, Stewart, *The Columbia,* op. cit. page 71.
8. Morgan, Margaret, *David Douglas, Botanist,* Honolulu, 1929. Page 39.
9. The Parker Ranch Museum, at Waimea on the island of Hawaii, had no reference to David Douglas, their most famous early visitor. It was on land now belonging to the Parker Ranch that Douglas was killed in 1834. See A. Grove Day, *Hawaii and its People,* New York, 1955, pages 173-174, for reference to the theory that Douglas was murdered rather than died accidentally.
10. Morgan, Margaret, op. cit. page 42.
11. Various newspaper accounts in Hawaii State Archives and in collections of the Hawaiian Historical Society. A bibliography of the Hawaiian language papers for the period is being edited by Clare Murdoch and will be published shortly by the historical society. These newspapers should contain information to supplement the English language newspapers' account of the funeral and burial of David Douglas, whose body was brought 300 miles by canoe from the island of Hawaii for interment in "the Missionary cemetery" at what is now Kawaiahao Church.
12. *William Fraser Tolmie, Physician and Fur Trader,* op. cit.
13. Ibid.
14. Reminiscence by his son, Simon Fraser Tolmie, which appears in the Appendix to *Physician and Fur Trader.*
15. Meeker, Ezra. *Tacoma Ledger,* May 22, 1892. Also see Meeker's *Pioneer Reminiscences,* Seattle, 1905, pages 446-449, for Tolmie's letter to Governor McMullen in behalf of Chief Leschi.
16. Tolmie's *Journal,* op. cit. James G. Swan was one of the most remarkable men in Washington Territory: collector, writer, artist, civil servant, teacher of the Indians. See *Almost out of the world: Scenes in Washington Territory,* by Swan, edited by W. A. Katz, published by the Washington State Historical Society in 1971; and *Swan among the Indians,* by Lucile McDonald, Portland, 1972.
17. *Our First Horticulturist,* Washington Historical Quarterly, Vols. 21-22.
18. Ibid. The original journal is in the manuscript collections of the Maryland Historical Society.
19. *The Great United States Exploring Expedition,* op. cit. page 259.
20. Ibid. Page 302.

Chapter Twelve, Scottish Gold

1. Jackson, W. Turrentine. *The Enterprising Scot*, Edinburgh, 1968. Page 19.
2. Ibid. Pages 24 ff.
3. op. cit. Pages 26-27.
4. 1978 marks the 400th anniversary of Drake's voyage to the Pacific Coast of America.
5. Among them, James Douglas, Dr. Tolmie, Robert Firth, and many others. See *Hudson's Bay Miscellany*, op. cit. page 221, footnote, and Tolmie's *Journal*, op. cit. Fort Nisqually and Cowlitz Farms were the key posts in the farm system. See also *Empire of the Columbia*, Johansen and Gates, pages 134-135, and 208-209.
6. Shafer, Gladys. Manuscript notes on Robert Firth, *Collections of the Washington State Historical Society*.
7. The Scottish Record Office contains records of the founding and operations of several of these companies, including the correspondence of the Sublettes, of the Rocky Mountain Fur Company, with Captain William Drummond Stewart. (Copies of these letters are in the Washington State Historical Society.)
8. *Orkney and Shetland American*, January, February 1888; October, 1890. There is also a copy of *The Shetland Times*, special edition, June 19, 1889, which contains a fascinating account of "The Hoswick Whale Dispute," a matter of interest to the Scots who left the islands for North America. The question was who owned title to a shoal of whales which were stranded near Lerwick, with 450 pounds, 12 shillings and one pence at stake!
9. Crick, Bernard. *A Guide to Manuscripts Relating to America in Great Britain and Ireland*, London, 1961. Pages 220-221; 341 fn.
10. After "the Clearances" began, Scottish farmers were eager targets for the promotional material put out by recruiters for America. See Bumgardner, Georgia, *American Broadsides*, Barre, 1971, for examples: Plate 5, *Information for Immigrants to the New-England States;* Plate 6, *Information, To those who are disposed to migrate to South-Carolina*, both dated 1795; Plate 7, *New Ohio Lands, and Title Indisputable.* Emigrants who had already settled in America were encouraged to write back to the British Isles about the golden opportunities. Crick lists and describes about 400 emigrant letters on pages 327-334, in *A Guide to Manuscripts Relating to America in Great Britain and Ireland*, op. cit.
11. Scottish interest in Alaska dated from the involvement of the Hudson's Bay Company with the Russian-American Company. The Puget Sound Agricultural Company was founded, in part, to enable the HBC to sell produce and goods to the Russians in Alaska. See Bancroft's *History of Alaska*, San Francisco, 1886. The official government *Report of the Population, Industries, and Resources of Alaska*, Washington, D.C. 1882, was read with eagerness in Europe while Americans were still calling the Alaska Purchase by the demeaning name, "Seward's Folly.' Not until the outbreak of the gold rush to Alaska in 1897 did Americans begin to awaken to the enormous potential of what would become the 49th state. One Scot, John Muir, saw its bounty as a great national resource which must be conserved, and so reported in *Travels in Alaska*, Boston, 1915. As stated in the text, no effort was made to include Alaska in this study of the Scot in the Pacific Northwest.

Bibliographical essay

Included here are sources which will be helpful to the scholar who wants to explore the subject of Scottish influence in northwest history beyond the limited scope of this book. I have listed far more than the archives, manuscripts, books and articles which were used in writing this study.

Manuscripts. The most important collections of fur trade history, and a rich source for study of the Scots who played key roles in the Pacific Northwest are in the archives of the Hudson's Bay Company in Winnipeg. The archives were moved there from Beaver House, in London, where they accumulated for 300 years, the transfer being made in 1970, the venerable Company's 300th anniversary. Such significant papers as those of Sir George Simpson, for nearly forty years North American Governor of the Company; the reports and letterbooks of Dr. John McLoughlin, Chief Factor at Fort Vancouver during the period when HBC controlled most of the Pacific Northwest; the records of the fifth Earl of Selkirk, when he served as Governor and encouraged the emigration to the Red River Colony; letterbooks and reports of Sir Charles Ross and Dr. William Fraser Tolmie. In fact, these are exemplary for all of the Hudson's Bay Company officers' records now in Company archives. Though the Hudson's Bay Record Society is publishing at stated intervals, it has been estimated roughly that publication of all of the records would take not less than 200 years!

Several universities and state historical societies have supplementary records of the northwest fur trade. There are important manuscripts in the Yale Collection of Western Americana; the Bancroft Library, at Berkeley; the Huntington Library, at San Marino; the University of Washington; Washington State University; the University of Oregon, and the University of British Columbia. Most have published inventories of the collections, some only in part. The collections of the Washington State Historical Society contain the papers of Hiram M. Chittenden, historian of the American fur trade; the Brewer letters, which shed much light on missionary-fur trader relationships (such as correspondence between Marcus Whitman, Fort Vancouver and Fort Walla); the diary of Narcissa Whitman, quoted extensively herein; the Archibald McKinlay papers; Peter Skene Ogden letters and a copy of his journal at New Caledonia; Letters from former colleagues, such as Dr. Tolmie, in the Thomas Chambers Collection; annotated original maps of the census of western Indian tribes by George Gibbs for Governor Isaac Stevens; many pioneer narratives, some of which were published in the *Tacoma Ledger* in the 1890's; copies of David Douglas letters and journals from Hawaii. There are other names, but this indicates the richness of the collections in Tacoma.

Similar holdings at the Oregon Historical Society, the Idaho Historical Society, the Montana Historical Society, and the Archives of British Columbia, are available for further research.

Exploration and Discovery. The original logs, journals, atlases, and letters of the earliest expeditions by sea from Europe are, as a rule, in the archives of London, Paris, Edinburgh, Leningrad, and Seville. Many of the voyages have been published in scholarly editions, such as J. C. Beaglehole's editions of the Cook journals, published by the Hakluyt Society. The rare pre-publication edition of Vancouver's *Voyages*, one of five sets prepared before the regular edition, will be published eventually in a facsimile edition by the Washington State Historical Society, owner of one of the sets. The journal of John Nicol, who was with Portlock, ran to more than 1,000 pages in the original manuscript, but was published most recently in an edition which was only 187 pages, and those in large type. If the original was not destroyed by the printer or editor what a treasure for some scholar to edit!

The Lewis and Clark Papers are in the American Philosophical Society, in Philadelphia, and the field notes for the expedition at Yale University. All have been published. However, several of the journals kept on the expedition have never been found, and may surface someday to throw new light on the epic journey.

The largest body of materials for the United States Exploring Expedition, or the Wilkes Expedition, is in the National Archives. Daniel Haskell's exhaustive bibliography, *The United States Exploring Expedition, 1838-1842, and Its Publications* is most useful in locating supplementary collections. William Stanton's *The Great United States Exploring Expedition,* published in 1975, lists the journals in other depositories, including the journal of William D. Brackenridge, at the Maryland Historical Society, the Colvocoresses journal at Yale, and the James Alden journal at the Mariners Museum, at Newport News. The Brackenridge journal was published by the Washington Historical Quarterly in Volumes 21 and 22, under the title of *Our First Official Horticulturist.*

Maritime history. Information about Scottish mariners in the northwest may be found in Lewis and Dryden's *Marine History of the Pacific Northwest,* Portland, 1905, with supplementary editions published by the Puget Sound Maritime Historical Society. The sources for the new editions were the Horace McCurdy Collection, Seattle Historical Society, and the Special Collections of the University of Washington. An unpublished history of the Sailors Union of the Pacific, by Ottilie Markholt, is in the Washington State Historical Society, but is restricted at present. *The Sea Chest,* published by the Puget Sound Maritime Historical Society, offers occasional useful memoirs of "Old Salts," an amazing number of whom are Scots. Frederick Howay's *A List of the Trading Vessels in the Maritime Fur Trade, 1795 to 1825,* an expanded version of his *An Outline Sketch of the Maritime Fur Trade,* in the *Annual Report* of the Canadian Historical Association, Toronto, 1932, has been revised and re-edited by Richard Pierce, and is a valuable reference for tracing Scots on early voyages to the Northwest Coast. Complementary to that volume is *Voyages to Hawaii before 1860,* edited by Judd and Lind, available from the University of Hawaii Press. This is a valuable aid, too, because most of the ships which visited the northwest during the heyday of the fur trade and the earlier period of discovery, also touched the Sandwich Islands, generally en route to China with furs or sandalwood. An excellent maritime bibliography can be checked in Barry Gough's *The Royal Navy and the Northwest Coast of North America,* Vancouver, 1791. Scots were well represented in the British Navy and the bibliography reflects the fact. Warren Cook's *Flood Tide of Empire: Spain and the Pacific Northwest,* Yale, 1973, also has a superb bibliography, though the emphasis is first upon the Spanish voyages, the subject of the book itself.

Agriculture. The first farms were operated by the Puget Sound Agricultural Company for the Hudson's Bay Company and the records are in the Company archives at Winnipeg. Dr. Tolmie's journal, cited herein, is a valuable report on farming at Fort Nisqually and Fort Victoria. Narcissa Whitman's journal gives a good account of farming operations at Fort Vancouver. *The History of Fort Vancouver and its Physical Structure,* by John Hussey, and published by the Washington State Historical Society, also includes descriptions of farming operations at Fort Vancouver.

A valuable source for additional information on HBC operations is the *Settlement of the Claims of the Puget Sound Agricultural Company,* a published account of the final arbitration between the United States and Great Britain following the settlement of the Oregon boundary question. The Washington State Historical Society has a complete set of the rare volumes.

Washington State University has specialized in collecting the agricultural history of the Inland Empire. Several theses have been published there and at the University of Washington which have valuable material on some of the Scots who pioneered farming, including the McGregor family. Oregon State University has also concentrated on the subject for Oregon. Both they and the Oregon Historical Society have interesting collections on fruit culture. A student of horticulture could begin with Menzies' unpublished journal, a copy of which is at the Archives of British Columbia, though the original is in the British Museum. The papers of David Douglas, in the Royal Horticultural Society, at Kew Gardens, are another rich resource. The files of *Agricultural History* contain occasional articles on northwest agriculture, such as *The Cattle Herds and Ranches of the Oregon Country*, 1860-1890, by J. Orin Oliphant, Vol. 21:4, October 1947. The importance of irrigation and power to northwest farms is explored by George Sundberg in *Hail Columbia: The Thirty Year Struggle for Grand Coulee Dam*. Judith Kenny explored *Early Sheep Ranching in Eastern Oregon*, in the Oregon Historical Quarterly, LXIV: 2, June 1963. Alfred L. Lomax followed the product to the *Pioneer Woolen Mills in Oregon*, 1811-1875 (Portland, 1941). The student should also explore the steamboat river navigation and the coming of the railroads with their impact upon northwest farming. One important manuscript collection for railroad history is the Major A. B. Rogers Collection, the papers of the man who surveyed railroad rights-of-way for the Canadian Pacific and the Great Northern. The collection is at the Washington State Historical Society. Randall V. Mills' *Sternwheelers up the Columbia: A Century of Steamboating in the Oregon Country*, and *Railroads down the Valleys: Some Short Lines of the Oregon Country* (Palo Alto 1947; Palo Alto 1950) are good beginnings on two important influences on northwestern agricultural development. Oscar Winther's *The Transportation Frontier: Trans-Mississippi West*, 1865-1890 is helpful, particularly in identifying the individuals associated with the development of the systems which moved farm goods to market.

Commercial Investment. The outstanding source book is *The Enterprising Scot*, by W. Turrentine Jackson. Originally published in Edinburgh, the book is now available in an American edition. Jackson's bibliography is admirable, listing most of the available resources and other studies. A book which complements *The Enterprising Scot* is *British Investments and the American Mining Frontier*, 1860-1901, by Clark Spence (Ithaca, 1958). The book includes the Scots among the British investors, but the mining operations which they subsidized were somewhat remote from the Pacific Northwest. This entire area of investigation presents a real challenge. As mentioned in the chapter *Scottish Gold*, one study could be made to determine connections between the Highland "Clearances" and the Dundee and Edinburgh investment companies promoting emigration to the United States. Another interesting project would be the promotional literature itself; the brochures, pamphlets, newspaper advertisements, which attempted to spur either emigration to the United States and the Pacific Northwest or to encourage investment in the developing frontier territories.

Literature and art. No in-depth effort was made for this book to find all of the artists or writers who came to the Pacific Northwest, or wrote or painted it, who were of Scottish birth or descent. This could be a fascinating project. The papers of Washington Irving and the John Jacob Astor Collection, upon which he based his *Astoria*, are in the New York Public Library. Irving's journal of a visit to Scotland, when he spent some time with Sir Walter Scott, is also there. Scott was then Europe's leading novelist, using Scottish history and folklore for his sources. Irving was just beginning to investigate the same kind of sources for American literature. Scott's example and literary success may have spurred him on, resulting not only in stories of Catskill Dutch, but to *Astoria* and *The Adventures of Captain Bonneville.*

Classified as a nature writer, John Muir was far more. The pioneer conservationist was a philosopher, a stylist, and an artist. This Scotsman's writings helped to create a national policy which saved Yosemite, Muir Woods, and other national parks for posterity, at a time when our timber resources were considered to be limitless. Muir's many trips into the northwest were inspired by his interests in forests and glaciers. His journals were edited in 1938 by Linnie Wolfe and published under the title *John of the Mountains.* W. F. Bade edited ten volumes of his writings, and also wrote *The Life and Letters of John Muir,* 2 vols. in 1923-1924.

James E. Stuart, the nephew of Gilbert Stuart, the famed painter of portraits, is not to be confused with the other James E. Stuart, better known as "Jeb" Stuart, of Civil War fame. The artist had a studio in the 1880's in Ashland, Oregon, in 1885 and, for several years after, in Portland. He finally moved to California, spending the rest of his life in Oakland and San Francisco. His magnificent landscapes and scenes of northwestern Indian life are treasured by museums. The Washington State Historical Society has fourteen of his paintings in its permanent collections.

Much needs to be done on the history of art in the Oregon country and, except for museum files, there are few published sources. Franz Stenzel's books on Cleveland Rockwell and James Alden are good beginnings (*Cleveland Rockwell, Scientist and Artist,* Portland 1972). *The New-York Historical Society's Dictionary of Artists in America,* 1564-1860 (Yale 1957) is useful for established names, but little help for lesser known artists of the Pacific Northwest. *National Parks and the American Landscape,* the Smithsonian Institution Press, 1972; *Mountains, Mules, Mosquitos and Men: The Sketchbook of Alfred Downing* (Bruce Le Roy, in *American Heritage,* February 1965); *Northwest History in Art,* 1778 to 1963, edited by Bruce Le Roy (Washington State Historical Society, 1967) a series of six catalogues of special exhibits of northwestern artists; *Lewis and Clark's America: A voyage of Discovery,* 2 vols. Seattle Art Museum, 1976. This catalogue contained a number of the sketches of Alfred Jacob Miller, who accompanied Sir William Drummond Stewart on his western trip in 1835, when the Scottish sportsman traveled with the fur brigades. *Artists of the Old West,* by John Ewers (Garden City, 1973); *Across the Wide Missouri,* by Bernard De Voto (Boston, 1947); *Artists and Illustrators of the old West,* 1850-1900, by Robert Taft (New York 1953). These books and catalogues provide a basic, even bare-bones beginning for the student who would trace the Scot as artist in the Pacific Northwest. Biographical data on such artists as William Keith, William Fife, John Mix Stanley and others who painted in Washington Territory is in preparation in a book in progress. Artists' letters or, even harder, diaries, are hard to find. The new Archives of American Art, in Detroit, is gathering such data as fast as it turns up, as are most historical societies in America.

General books. A useful model is *The Scottish Tradition in Canada,* by W. Stanford Reid (Toronto, 1976). Having been written by fourteen authorities on various phases of Scottish customs, the book is over-solemn but an impressive collation, all in all. An interesting but hard to find book is *The Scots Book,* which is a compendium of facts, folklore, and quotations. It was published in London in 1935, and was compiled and edited by Ronald Macdonald Douglas, a very respectable name indeed. There are numberless histories of Scotland, and guides to her various regions. There is no point in listing them here, except to note that the currently accepted best general history of Scotland is *A Short History of Scotland,* by R. L. Mackie, rev. ed., edited by G. Donaldson. For the serious student, *Scotland from the Earliest Times to* 1603, by W. C. Dickinson, and *Scotland from* 1603 *to the Present Day,* by G. S. Pryde. *A Source Book of Scottish History,* 3 vols. 2nd ed., by W. C. Dickinson, G. Donaldson, and I. A. Milne, covers the period from the earliest times to 1707. *Scotland in Modern Times,* 1720-1939, by A. M. Mackenzie, supplements the preceding volume. What occurred between 1707 and 1720, the 13 year gap between these volumes, can be found in other sources. The historical literature on Scotland would make a vast collection, with individual periods and subjects well covered. The above listing is only a recommended beginning. *The Scot in History,* by Wallace Notestein, published in 1970 from the Yale edition of 1946, is an invaluable corollary study. Before one can know what the Scot became in America one must learn what he *was,* and why he left Scotland. Thus the above listing.

Folklore. The literature concerning the folkways of the Scot in America may be found in scattered sources. Before reading the masterwork, *The English and Scottish Popular Ballads,* by Francis J. Child, the reader should be familiar with the classic Percy *Folio,* the *Reliques of Ancient English Poetry,* published in 1765, which stimulated ballad research. The name is a misnomer, since the *Reliques* contain many Scots ballads. Child's ballad collection, published from 1882 to 1898, paralleled the beginning of the *Journal of American Folklore,* the official organ of the American Folklore Society, in 1888. The journal has carried the reports of folklorists who worked in folk song research from that day to this. Many articles on Scottish ballads and folksongs have appeared in the past ninety years in the pages of the Journal. Indexes are available.

Another classic which preceded Child by eighty years is Sir Walter Scott's *Minstrelsy of the Scottish Border.* One should read the work for flavor, for the masterful notes and introduction, but always bearing in mind that Scott was a poet more than a critic. When a word or phrase didn't satisfy his poetic instincts, he changed it. This is a cardinal sin where the true folklorist is concerned, equivalent to changing style or grammar in a diary for the historian. But the *Minstrelsy* is a great book and should be read as literature, if not historical accuracy. Scott went on to use many of the ballad themes in his novels: historic battles, clan history, witchcraft, tales of supernatural assignation, etc. His justification may be found in the final paragraph to his introduction to the *Minstrelsy,* and it says something applicable to our study of the Scot in northwest America: "By such efforts, feeble as they are, I may contribute somewhat to the history of my native country; the peculiar features of whose manners and character are daily melting and dissolving into those of her sister and ally." "Her sister and ally," of course, was England. Something of the same certainly applies to the Scot who emigrated to America, his folkways, including folk songs and ballads, changing or melting away. Paradoxically, Professor Child, and after him, Cecil Sharp, found that many of the songs lived on in the southeastern United States which had been lost to tradition in the British Isles. The isolation of the Scottish settlements in Appalachia had much to do with it.

One of the best references to folksong and balladry in the United States is *Native American Balladry, a Descriptive Study and a Bibliographical Syllabus,* by G. Malcolm Laws. Here are listed the best guides to regional folksong: Brown's *Collection of North Carolina Folklore;* Flanders' *The New Green Mountain Songster;* Korson's *Coal Dust on the Fiddle,* and *Minstrels of the Mine Patch;* Leach's *The Ballad*

Book; Lomax, *The Folk Songs of North America;* Mackenzie, *The Quest of the Ballad;* Randolph, *Ozark Folksongs;* Thompson, *Body, Boots and Britches,* and *A Pioneer Songster;* Wells, *The Ballad Tree.* There are many more, but these would give the student a good start. Almost every one of the titles cited above contains information about Scots ballads and the widely scattered regions where they may be found in the oral tradition. Moore's *Ballads and Songs of the Southwest* could be added, though the book draws heavily on Hispanic tradition. Bruce Le Roy's *The Bold Northwestman: Folk Songs and Ballads of the Pacific Northwest* is a work in progress, parts of which have been published separately. The book is the first to deal exclusively with the folk songs of the Northwest.

Books which contain material on witchcraft, demonology and the supernatural, Scottish style, are generally only popular treatments, such as *The Scots Week-End,* by Donald and Catherine Carswell; *Selected Highland Folktales* and *More Highland Folktales,* by R. Macdonald Robertson, published by Oliver and Boyd, of Edinburgh, is excellent, if a popular approach; *Tales of the Covenanters,* by Robert Pollok, published by John Ritchie, of Kilmarnock, Scotland, is the reprint of a study written eighty years ago, but still a good source about the days of "the Risings," and the religious strife which rent Scotland. There are many articles about Scottish superstitions in the *Journal of American Folklore.*

Proverbial sayings of the Scot, from which I drew several examples in this study, are listed in *Scottish Proverbs,* by James Kelly, and the edition I used was published in Edinburgh in 1718, but the book appeared in a limited edition many years before that.

Biographical. A number of the people listed in *Fifty Scots in Northwest History,* have been the subject of biographies which I will not list by title. They include George Abernethy, William Clark, James Cook, George Crook, Alexander Dalrymple, George Davidson, David Douglas, James Douglas, Abigail Scott Duniway, U. S. Grant, John Paul Jones, Alexander Mackenzie, Morton Matthew McCarver, Ranald MacDonald, John McLoughlin, John Muir, Archibald Menzies, Peter Skene Ogden, Alexander Ross, Sir George Simpson, William Fraser Tolmie, and William Wallace. Sources of information about the rest included Lewis and Dryden's *Marine History of the Pacific Northwest;* Elwood Evans' *History of the Pacific Northwest;* Stewart Holbrook's *The Columbia;* Philip Cogswell's *Capitol Names: Individuals Woven into Oregon's History;* Edward Eberstadt's *The Northwest Coast;* and a variety of county and state histories (sometimes called the "Mug Books").

HBC *Beaver* at Steilacoom — Kenn Johnson

Fifty Scots in northwest history

1. *Abernethy, George* — First Governor of Oregon Provisional government. Born in Aberdeen, Scotland, 1807. Family moved to United States and lived in New York state. At 33 years of age Abernethy came to Oregon as a lay member of the Methodist mission. At Oregon City he managed the Mission store. When the Provisional government was organized in 1845 he was chosen as governor, serving until Oregon Territory was established in 1849. Later engaged in business at Oregon City and Linn City. After the flood of 1861 at Oregon City he moved to Portland. He died in 1877.

2. *Barclay, Forbes* — Chief physician for Hudson's Bay Company in 1839 at Fort Vancouver; civic leader Oregon City, where he moved in 1850. Born in 1812, Lerwick, Shetland Islands; died 1873. In Arctic search for Sir John Ross in 1831. Married Marie Pambrun, daughter of Pierre Pambrun, HBC chief trader, Columbia district. Barclay House, in Oregon City, is maintained as a museum.

3. *Barlow, Samuel Kimbrough* — Oregon pioneer; born in Kentucky, 1795, of Scottish parents; explored and laid out original Barlow Road eighty miles long, pioneer passage which became a toll road during the Provisional government of Oregon, and was also a primary emigrant trail. (See pages 202-206, Evans.) He died at Oregon City in 1867.

4. *Birnie, James* — Fur trader, founder of Cathlamet, Washington. Born in Paisley, Scotland, 1800. Employed first by North West Company in 1818, then by Hudson's Bay Company at Fort Vancouver, 1825-1831. Built Fort Simpson, returned to Astoria where he ran a trading post. In 1845 he settled on present site of Cathlamet. His historic home is now occupied by Julia Butler Hansen, former Congresswoman from Washington State.

5. *Brackenridge, William Dunlop* — Botanist on Wilkes U.S. Exploring Expedition; born in Scotland in 1810; died near Baltimore, 1893. Four years with Wilkes Expedition, his Puget Sound journal appeared in the Washington Historical Quarterly, under the title *Our First Official Horticulturist;* WHQ vols. 21 and 22. See chapter *Botanizing Scots.*

6. *Chadwick, Stephen* — Fifth Governor of Oregon. Born 1825 in Middletown, Connecticut, of Scottish and English descent. Came to Oregon in 1851, where he practiced law; secretary of state 1870-1878, became governor in 1877, serving during Nez Perce War. Died in Salem, Oregon in 1895.

7. *Campbell, Alexander Colin* — Farmer, miner, banker. Born in 1833 in Perth, Ontario, Canada, of Donald and Mary McCoy Campbell, emigrants from Scotland. He was a pioneer hop-grower, followed the Fraser River mining gold rush in 1862. Helped to organize the National Bank of Commerce, in Tacoma, became president of the Farmers' Bank, of Puyallup. Served as mayor of Puyallup. He died in 1894.

8. *Christie, James* — Explorer of Olympic peninsula. Born in Moray, Scotland, 1851, and came to Canada in 1871. Served as a soldier with the Canadian Artillery from Quebec to Manitoba until 1876 when he joined the Mounted Police for special service. Met the Indian warriors under Sitting Bull when they fled to Canada after the Custer Battle of the Little Big Horn. During the Riel Rebellion he served at the Military Colonization Ranch near Calgary. He explored the Arctic for three years, prospecting as he went. In December, 1889, he led the Seattle Press Expedition into the Olympic wilderness for six months of exploration. This

story is told in *Untamed Olympics,* by Ruby El Hult; *Name Calling on the Olympic Peninsula,* by Robert Hitchman; and *Across the Olympic Mountains: The Press Expedition, 1889-1890,* by Robert L. Wood. Later he settled in Vernon, British Columbia, where he alternated farming and prospecting, as well as working for Indian rights. He died in 1942 at the age of 91.

9. *Clark, William* — Explorer and co-commander of Lewis and Clark Expedition. Born in 1770 in Caroline County, Virginia, the younger brother of General George Rogers Clark, conqueror of British posts in the west during the American Revolution. Their parents were of Scottish descent. Appointed by Thomas Jefferson to share command of first United States exploring expedition from St. Louis to the mouth of the Columbia River, 1803-1806. Gave the United States its major claim to Oregon territory, opening the northwest for the overland fur trade, eventual settlement.

10. *Cook, James* — World's greatest explorer; born in 1728, in Marton-in-Cleveland, Yorkshire, the son of a Lowland Scot farm laborer who emigrated to England after the Jacobite rebellion of 1715. Cook made three great voyages, the third and last being one when he discovered and charted the northwest coast of North America. His published journals revealed the rich harvest of sea otter to be gleaned on the northwest coast, with subsequent great profit in China. This news precipitated the "fur rush" which led to exploration, exploitation and eventual settlement of the previously unknown region. He died in Hawaii in 1779, in a skirmish with natives on Kealakekua Bay. See chapter *From the Heather to the Sea.*

11. *Crook, George* — Soldier and Indian fighter. Born in Dayton, Ohio in 1829 of Scottish and German ancestry. Served from 1852 until 1860 in the Oregon country, being involved in many skirmishes between the Indians and the white settlers in the Yakima area, the Rogue River, and along the Oregon coast. Served the Union during the Civil War, where he attained the rank of major-general. Returned to the Oregon country in 1871 where he helped to settle the Bannock-Piute war. He died in Chicago in 1890.

12. *Crooks, Ramsay* — Born in Scotland in 1787, this pioneer fur-trader joined the Astor party in 1811. He led his group through the Snake River country, enduring great privations. Crooks returned east in 1813, continuing as a partner of John Jacob Astor in St. Louis and New York until 1834 when he purchased and became president of the American Fur Company. He died in 1859.

13. *Dalrymple, Alexander* — Geographer. Born in 1737 in New Hailes, Scotland. Though never in America, Dalrymple served with the East India Company at Madras, where he became hydrographer to the Company in 1779. Appointed hydrographer to the British Admiralty which he served until his death in 1808. He was responsible for preparing and publishing the reports of Captain Cook's third voyage which had tremendous impact upon the opening of the northwest.

14. *Davidson, George* — Geologist, geographer, astronomer. Born in England in 1825, of Scottish parents. Davidson conducted geodetic surveys of the Pacific Coast for the U.S. Coast Survey in 1850. He published the *Directory of the Pacific Coast of the United States* which became the *Pacific Coast Pilot,* considered the most accurate guide from then to now. He was a founder of the Geographic Society of the Pacific. He died in 1911.

15. *Douglas, David* — Naturalist, explorer, author. Born in Perthshire, Scotland, in 1798. From 1825 to 1833 Douglas visited and explored the Pacific Northwest

three times. On these trips he discovered more than fifty varieties of trees, of which the best known is what we call "the Douglas fir," though its scientific name is *pseudotsuga Taxifolia*. His exploits are described in a chapter in this book, *Botanizing Scots*. He was killed accidentally in Hawaii in 1834. His journals have been published and are fascinating reading.

16. *Douglas, James* — Fur trader, Governor of Vancouver Island. Born in 1803, Lanarkshire, Scotland; Chief Factor, Fort Vancouver, where he succeeded John McLoughlin. One of the founders of Victoria, he moved there in 1849 after the settlement of the Hudson's Bay Company claims. He became the second governor of Vancouver Island, serving until 1858. From 1859 to 1863 he served as the first governor of British Columbia. Douglas kept a cool head during the "Pig War" dispute over San Juan Island, averting general war with the United States. Died 1877.

17. *Duniway, Abigail Scott* — Born in 1834 in Groveland, Illinois, she was the daughter of John Tucker Scott, of Scottish descent. A pioneer fighter for women's suffrage, Mrs. Duniway edited *The New Northwest* which helped to publicize the cause. Her work in Washington and Oregon helped bring passage of suffrage amendments to the state constitutions. An indefatigible lecturer, Mrs. Duniway worked closely with national suffrage leaders, but her personal dynamism won the vote for women in her adopted state. She died in Portland in 1915.

18. *Eldridge, Edward* — Pioneer settler, one of founders of Bellingham, Washington. Born in St. Andrews, Scotland, in 1792 (according to his son, Hugh Eldridge; Elwood Evans lists his birth date as 1828, probably an error). Shipped out of Scotland at age 11, as a cabin boy. He became a licensed navigator, making his first trip to America in 1846. He sailed as a crew member on the Great Lakes for awhile, but returned to the high seas, putting in at San Francisco in 1849, at the beginning of the gold rush. After a year at mining he returned to sea, serving in coastwise service between San Francisco and Panama. On one of these trips he met Captain Henry Roeder who had built a sawmill on Bellingham Bay. On his advice, Eldridge came to Bellingham, taking up a land claim of 320 acres adjoining Roeder's site. He served during the Indian War of 1855 under command of Major Van Bokkelen. He was a member of the legislature, becoming speaker of the House in 1866-1867, and in 1878 was a member of the territorial constitutional convention. When Bellingham became an incorporated townsite, Eldridge's land became a part of the original platted site. (See Evans, pages 316-317; also *Told by the Pioneers*, vol. 2, pages 130-131.) Eldridge died in 1892.

19. *Firth, Robert* — Born in 1830, in the Orkney Islands, this pioneer farmer entered service with the Hudson's Bay Company in 1849. He was employed on the Company farms at Victoria for several years, but was transferred to San Juan Island in 1862. Here he raised sheep and cattle to supply company posts. After withdrawal of American troops who had been stationed on the Island during the "Pig War," he occupied Captain Pickett's house. The Hudson's Bay Company turned over its island property to him after San Juan Island was awarded to the United States. He lived there until his death in 1903.

20. *Gairdner, Meredith* — Physician for the Hudson's Bay Company; born in Edinburgh in 1809. Sailed with Dr. William Fraser Tolmie in 1833 to Fort Vancouver, answering a request by Dr. John McLoughlin to the Company for medical assistants. Served at Fort Vancouver until 1836 when he sailed to the Sandwich Islands (Hawaii) in an effort to recuperate from an illness. He died there in 1837 at the

age of 28. During his stay at Fort Vancouver, he, like Tolmie, studied botany and Indian customs. In 1835 he stole Chief Comcomly's skull and shipped it to England. There are conflicting stories as to why he did this, but the fact that the skull was flattened probably piqued his professional interest.

21. *Grant, Ulysses S.* — Frontier soldier, Civil War general, President. Born in 1822 at Point Pleasant, Ohio, Grant was the direct descendant of Matthew Grant who emigrated from Scotland to Dorchester, Massachusetts, in 1630. Served at Fort Vancouver from 1852 to 1854 where he was regimental quartermaster for the Fourth Infantry. Here he speculated in a foredoomed business of shipping ice south to San Francisco, planted a large potato garden which was flooded out, ordered chickens and shipped them to San Francisco. The chickens all died en route. Harrassed by Captain George McClellan for whom he was ordered to outfit a surveying party, Grant took to drink. Not long after, Grant resigned from the Army, considering himself a total failure, since his business ventures had not helped him to raise enough money to bring Mrs. Grant and their children out from the east. The application for his resignation was approved by Secretary of War Jefferson Davis in 1854. Not many years later, he would be appointed Commander of the Union forces. In 1868, he was elected President of the United States. Grant County, Washington, was named in his honor in 1908, memorializing the general and the President, rather than the ill-fated potato farmer of Fort Vancouver.

22. *Irving, William* — Ship's captain. Born in Annan, Dumfrieshire, Scotland, in 1816. First arrived in Oregon in 1849 as master and part owner of the barkentine *Success* with which he entered coastal trade. Purchased a little steam boat, the *Eagle,* which he brought to Portland on the deck of the *Success,* then used her in the Portland to Oregon City run. Finally owner of a number of pioneer steamers, several used in river traffic. In 1858 he sold his interests and went to British Columbia, where he joined Alexander Murray, building the first steamboat in British Columbia, the *Governor Douglas.* He also built the *Colonel Moody,* making the first successful trip to Yale in 1861. He later built and operated other steamboats in British Columbia. He died at New Westminster, B.C. in 1872.

23. *Jones, John Paul* — Father of American Navy. Born Kirkbean, Kirkcudbright, Scotland, in 1747. See chapter *A Journey Home* for theory as to how he may have influenced the Selkirk emigration to North America (present Alberta) and Canada, later to Puget Sound and Willamette Valley. Died in Paris, France, 1792.

24. *MacGrimmon, J. C.* — Yakima Valley pioneer. Born in the Isle of Skye, Scotland, in 1848. Sailed to California at the age of thirteen, "to seek his fortune." After three years in San Francisco, he moved to Victoria where he worked for Wells, Fargo & Company. Followed the gold rush to the Caribou in 1866, later worked mines on the Arctic Circle, spending his winters in Victoria. Worked on the building of the Oregon Railway & Navigation Company, Cascade Division, in 1883 superintending the grading of the division. In 1884 he moved to Yakima, and entered the general merchandise business. In 1888, he sold his interest, purchased land and went into real estate and the business of raising apples. His apple ranch was one of the most successful in an area which is now known as "the Fruit Bowl of the nation."

25. *Mackenzie, Alexander* — Explorer, fur trader. Born in Stornoway, the Hebrides, 1763. Mackenzie was the first white man to reach the Pacific Coast overland, in 1798. He was a partner in the North West Company. He also explored to the

Arctic Ocean. His journals were published as *Voyages from Montreal, on the River St. Lawrence, through the Continent of North America, to the Frozen and Pacific Oceans, in the years* 1789 *and* 1793. Died in 1820.

26. *McCarver, Morton Matthew* — Founder of Sacramento and Tacoma; born in Lexington, Kentucky, 1807. He came over the Oregon Trail in 1843, taking up a claim on the Columbia River. First speaker of the house of the Oregon Provisional Legislature. In 1848 went to California gold rush, founded the city of Sacramento in 1849. He purchased a packet, the *Ocean Bird*, and brought many passengers north to Portland. In 1868, he founded Tacoma, Washington. He died in 1875.

27. *MacDonald, Ranald* — World traveler. Born in Astoria in 1824, the son of Archibald MacDonald, Factor of the Hudson's Bay Company post at Astoria, and husband of Princess Raven, the daughter of Chinook Chief Comcomly. Comcomly greeted both the Astor Expedition and the Lewis and Clark Expedition. Attended schools at Fort Vancouver and at Winnipeg. In 1848, he shipped out as a deck hand on a whaling ship bound for the Sea of Japan. When off the northern tip of the island of Hokkaido, he paid the ship's captain for a 27 foot sailboat, a quadrant, and provisions, and set sail for the nearest island. After three days, within sight of land, he deliberately scuttled his craft. His goal had been to see Japan, a nation still isolated from the western world and determined to keep it that way. Taken as a prisoner to Nagasaki, he was finally allowed books and was permitted to instruct the Japanese in English. Some of his students became interpreters when Commodore Perry arrived in 1854. After nine months, MacDonald was deported aboard an American ship. After he reached home he began a series of mining and business ventures, none successful. His memoirs were written during his retirement near Kettle Falls, Washington. They have been published by the Eastern Washington State Historical Society. He died in 1894, at the age of 70, near Fort Colville.

28. *McKinlay, Archibald* — Fur trader, pioneer settler. Born in Perthshire, Scotland, about 1816, McKinlay served as Factor at Fort Walla Walla from 1841-1846, leaving for Oregon City just a few months prior to the Whitman Massacre at nearby Waiilatpu. He was married to Sarah Ogden, daughter of famed HBC Factor, Peter Skene Ogden. In 1862, he moved to Lac La Hache, British Columbia, where he ran a farm until his death in 1885.

29. *McKenzie, Donald* — Fur trader. Born in 1783 in Scotland. A partner of John Jacob Astor, he led the Astor Party to Oregon in 1812. Later he led trading and exploring expeditions up the Willamette, Columbia, Snake and McKenzie Rivers. The latter river was named for him. In 1813, to avoid seizure by the British he sold Astoria to the North West Company, but returned in employment of that firm. He was married to Princess Choim, a daughter of Chief Comcomly. He died in 1851.

30. *McLoughlin, John* — Fur trader, empire builder. Born in Riviere du Loup, Quebec, (his mother was Angelique Fraser whose parents came from Scotland) in 1784. His capsule biography is a chapter in this book (see *White-Headed Eagle*). He died in Oregon City in 1857 where McLoughlin House is maintained as an impressive memorial to the man they called "the Father of Oregon."

31. *McGilvery, Napoleon* — Soldier, miner, farmer. Born in 1825 at the Lake of the Woods, Upper Canada, at the Hudson's Bay post where his father was an officer. In 1839 he came to Vancouver where he was employed at the Fort until

1844, at which time he took up a homestead claim at Howell's Prairie. Served with Fremont in the Bear Flag Rebellion, in California, in 1846. He campaigned from Monterey to Los Angeles, helping to capture San Luis Obispo. In 1848, after an overland trip to Missouri with Commodore Stockton, he returned to Vancouver, but left at once for the California gold rush, where he remained two years at the mines. In California he guided the Argonauts between San Francisco and Sacramento. He finally returned to Oregon, where in 1853, he married Sarah Flett, daughter of William Flett, a member of the Red River expedition. He bought a large farm near Vancouver, Washington, where he died in 1906.

32. *McMillen, James H.* — Pioneer, Captain in Cayuse War, publisher; born in New York state, 1823. His great-grandfather emigrated from Scotland to Rhode Island; his grandfather moved to Attica, New York, where James was born. McMillen's family moved again to Du Page County, Illinois, where they had a farm. In 1845 James joined the great migration to Oregon, where he first found employment at Abernethy's mills in Oregon City. At the outbreak of the Cayuse War, which followed the Whitman Massacre, he joined the militia, or Oregon Volunteers, and occupied The Dalles. In 1851, he secured a donation land claim on the Tualatin Plains, where he farmed for a number of years. He was active in Republican party politics, held a number of civic offices, and made many philanthropic contributions. For some time, he served as president of the North Pacific History Company which published Elwood Evans' *History of the Pacific Northwest*. He died in 1913.

33. *Minto, John* — Pioneer farmer, orchardist. Born in 1822 in Newcastle-on-Tyne, England, the grandson of a Scot. His family emigrated to the United States in 1840, settling at Pittsburgh, Pennsylvania. John left for Oregon in 1844 in the company of Captain Cornelius Gilliam. He and two other young men in the party preceded the large band to the Willamette valley, then, with a *bateau* and provisions from John McLoughlin, returned to rescue an almost starving emigrant party. Settling near Salem, Minto experimented with fruit, grains, sheep raising, and was active in organizing the first Farmers' Club in Oregon. He also helped to locate the Cascade pass through which the Oregon Pacific Railroad built its line. During the Nez Perce War of 1877 he made a dangerous trip to the Snake River country with arms for General Oliver Otis Howard. Minto also cooperated in the promotion of emigration to Oregon, working as one of the directors of the Willamette *Farmer* and the Oregon Agricultural Society. He died in 1915.

34. *Muir, John* — Naturalist, explorer, author. Born in Dunbar, Scotland in 1838, Muir came to America in 1849. He was active in early western conservation efforts, influencing the development of the National Park system. His range was from the California Sierra to the mountains of Alaska. Yosemite National Park, Muir Woods, Muir glacier, (the latter in Alaska) are living memorials to this great naturalist whose writings influenced national policy and marked a pioneer substantial effort to preserve our western wilderness. He died in Los Angeles in 1914.

35. *Menzies, Archibald* — Botanist, author. Born in Perthshire, Scotland in 1754. Menzies was educated at the University of Edinburgh. He was employed as a surgeon by Captain George Vancouver and with him explored the Pacific Northwest in 1792. His journal is considered to be the best report of the Vancouver Expedition. During his visit to Puget Sound he discovered and named many new botan-

ical specimens. He died at Notting Hill, England in 1842. See chapter *Botanizing Scots.*

36. *Murray, Alexander Sinclair* — Pioneer ship's captain, ship builder, miner. Born in Scotland in 1827. At age 16 he left an apprenticeship in a lawyer's office, and sailed for Australia. News of the California gold rush lured him to San Francisco in 1849. After working on the Sacramento for awhile, he traded a ship's long-boat which he had used to ferry miners, for a larger boat. Making money on this venture, he purchased a brig and sailed for Sydney via Hawaii. On the re-turn trip, the vessel was wrecked. Eventually, by way of Australia, he again returned to the Pacific Coast. He spent some time at Salem, then purchased the *Washington,* which he placed in river traffic at Portland. Soon he built the *Port-land,* and acquired shares in four steamers. When the Fraser River gold rush began, Murray left the Columbia and Willamette river traffic and went north to British Columbia. Here he built the *Governor Douglas,* a steamer, at Victoria, the first steamer to be constructed in British Columbia. The following year, he constructed the *Colonel Moody,* in partnership with Captain William Irving who also had an interest in the earlier ship. Murray left British Columbia for Austra-lia again, where he pioneered steamboating on the Murray River in 1861. He also went to New Zealand where he built the *Tuape Ka.* His home base con-tinued to be Sydney, Australia until his death (date unknown). He was the Scot-seaman-promoter, *par excellence.*

37. *Nesmith, James* — Senator, Indian fighter. Born in New Brunswick, Canada, in 1820, Nesmith was of Ulster Scot descent. Educated in New England and Ohio, he moved to Iowa in 1842, planning to join an Oregon-bound party. For a short while journeyman carpenter at Fort Scott, he finally came on to Oregon in the large party led by Dr. Marcus Whitman in 1843. He took a donation land claim in Polk County in 1846; served as captain in the Cayuse Indian war in 1847-1848. In 1848, he went to California seeking gold, but returned the following year to build a flour mill near Dallas, Oregon. He also took part in the Rogue River Indian War in 1853, and served as a colonel in the Yakima Indian War, in 1855. He was appointed Superintendent of Indian Affairs in 1857, and was elected United States Senator from Oregon, serving from 1861 to 1865. He retired to his farm in 1867, but emerged to be elected to the House of Representatives 1873-1875. He died in 1885 near Dallas. A master of political invective. (See broad-side reproduced on a page herein.)

38. *Nicol, John* — Seaman, explorer, author. Born in Currie, near Edinburgh, in 1755. Sailed as a member of the crew of the *King George,* Captain Nathaniel Portlock commanding, in 1785. His *The Life and Adventures of John Nicol, Mariner* is an entertaining account of the events which led up to the Nootka Sound Controversy, at which time England nearly went to war with Spain over control of the North-west Coast. Nicol's adventurous life saw service in the American Revolution, the West Indies, trips to China and the Far East, whaling voyages, and the war be-tween France and England between 1794 and 1801. See chapter *From the Heath-er to the Sea.* He died in 1825, in Edinburgh.

39. *Ogden, Peter Skene* — Factor Hudson's Bay Company, explorer. Born in Quebec in 1794. His manuscript letters sometimes contain the spelling of "Skeen" for the second name. Probably one of the greatest figures in fur trade history, Ogden began with the North West Company in 1810, and was sent to the Columbia district in 1818. After the Company merged with the Hudson's Bay Company in

1821, he continued with the new company. He led many exploring expeditions, particularly notable being the one to the Snake River. Among the first to see the Great Salt Lake, in Utah, and the city of Ogden is named in his honor. Ogden's explorations covered the west. In 1845 he was appointed as Chief Factor of Fort Vancouver. He was instrumental in ransoming the survivors of the Whitman Massacre. He died at Oregon City in 1854.

40. *Reed, Walter J.* — Soldier, investor, town founder. Born near Edinburgh in 1842. His parents emigrated to America when he was six years old, living first in Ohio, then moving to Maryland where his father became superintendent of mines at Cumberland. The family moved again to Ohio, then Pennsylvania, where the father operated mines. In 1861 Reed enlisted in the Union army, serving in many campaigns and being wounded at Gettysburg. Both his father and brother also enlisted and both died in Confederate prison camps. Following the war, Reed came to California but shortly after moved to the Yakima country. In 1886 he took up a pre-emption claim at the present site of Cle Elum. Here he built the Reed House, a well-known hotel in that time, and located the coal fields near Roslyn and Cle Elum. He became wealthy through investing in the mining operations and running the best hotel in the area. He died in 1908.

41. *Reid, William* — Land developer, financier. Born in Glasgow, Scotland, in 1844. Educated in law at the University of Glasgow. Acting as vice-consul for the United States in Dundee, he became interested in the possibilities of Oregon for investment purposes. Active with the Oregon and Washington Trust and Investment Company, for which he served as secretary after his arrival in Portland in 1874. He organized the first savings bank in Oregon, built flour mills, purchased the Narrow Gauge Railroad for his company. For his promotional skills he became known in Oregon as "Dundee" Reid. He also organized the first Portland Board of Trade. He died in 1914. See chapter *Scottish Gold.*

42. *Ross, Alexander* — Fur trader, author. Born in 1783, in Nairnshire, Scotland. He emigrated to Canada in 1804 and was a school teacher in Montreal until 1810 when he was employed as a clerk for the Pacific Fur Company, owned by John Jacob Astor. He sailed on the *Tonquin*, the ill-fated ship which would later be destroyed in a battle with the Indians of Vancouver Island. He helped to build Fort Astoria after their arrival at the mouth of the Columbia, and later supervised the building of Fort Okanogan. After the demise of American control at Astoria during the War of 1812, he rejoined the management of the now Fort George, operated by the North West Company. From here he went to Fort Nez Perces in 1818, and remained in command of the post until 1823. He led an expedition into the Snake River country, going as far east as the site of present Boise, Idaho. The following year he took his family to the Red River Colony, near present-day Winnipeg. Here he received a grant of 100 acres and was appointed the first sheriff. He wrote three important books about his colorful career: *Adventures of the First Settlers on the Oregon or Columbia River* (London, 1849); *The Fur Hunters of the Far West* (1855); and *The Red River Settlement* (1856). He died at Red River in 1856.

43. *Ross, Charles* — Factor, Hudson's Bay Company. Born in 1794 in Scotland, Ross emigrated to North America in 1818. He served as chief clerk of the post at Fort Nisqually, then at Fort Victoria until his death in 1844. Ross came south from the Red River Colony in 1841. He has numerous descendants living in the Tacoma area today, including his great-grandson, Mr. E. K. Murray.

114

44. *Scott, Harvey Whitefield* — Editor, author. Born in 1838 in Illinois, of Scottish descent, the brother of Abigail Scott Duniway, the pioneer suffragette. He came to Oregon with his parents in 1852, losing his mother and his youngest brother while en route on the Oregon Trail. The family first settled in Oregon City but moved within two years near Shelton, in Washington Territory. Scott served with the Oregon Volunteers during the Yakima Indian War in 1855-1856. Upon discharge, he entered Pacific University but had to leave the following Spring for financial reasons. After two years of work, he re-entered the University and completed the course for graduation in 1863. For awhile he studied law while serving as librarian of the Portland Library. He became a regular contributor for the *Oregonian*. In 1865 he became editor of the paper. He was admitted to the Oregon Bar in the same year. Appointed U.S. Collector of Customs for Oregon 1870-1876, he returned to the *Oregonian* as editor and part-owner in 1877. He served as president of the Lewis and Clark Exposition 1903-1904. Mount Scott in Portland is named for him. He died in 1910.

45. *Selkirk, Earl of* — Hudson's Bay Company Governor, emigration promoter, author. Born in 1771 at St. Mary's Isle, Kirkcudbright, Scotland. Impressed by Commodore John Paul Jones who raided the Selkirk estate in 1778. Later, he financed the emigration of Scottish yeoman farmers to the Red River Colony in Canada. From that colony a number of families migrated to Puget Sound and the Willamette valley. (See chapter *A Journey Home.*) Thomas Douglas, the Fifth Earl of Selkirk, was the author of the two very important books on the Scottish emigration to North America: *Observations on the Present State of the Highlands of Scotland, with a View of the Causes and Probable Consequences of Emigration* (London, 1805); and *A Sketch of the British Fur Trade in North America; with Observations Relative to the North-West Company of Montreal* (London, 1816). He died and was buried at Pau, in France, in 1820.

46. *Simpson, Sir George* — Hudson's Bay Company Governor. Born about 1787 in Ross-shire, Scotland. Young George was apprenticed to a firm of importers and brokers in London but joined the Hudson's Bay Company in 1820. His first assignment was as a fur trader in the Athabasca department but after only a year he was promoted to Governor of the Pacific area. Energetic beyond belief, Simpson traveled to most of the posts under his command, going by the fast fur brigade canoes which visited all areas of the northwest. He selected the site for Fort Vancouver, with John McLoughlin, placing great authority in the man and the headquarters on the Columbia, an important factor in the development of the vast region under Company control. (For Simpson's methods of travel, see chapter *The Women*, for the accounts by Frances Simpson, the governor's young bride.) Simpson died in Lachine, Quebec, in 1860.

47. *Stuart, David* — Fur trader, Astor partner. Born in Perthshire, Scotland, in 1765. Sailed to Oregon aboard *Tonquin*, simultaneously with Alexander Ross. One of the builders and founders of Fort Astoria. He also established Fort Okanogan in 1811, the first American settlement in the present state of Washington. He died in 1853.

48. *Tolmie, William Fraser* — Physician, botanist, author, legislator. Born at Inverness, Scotland, in 1812. Came on to Pacific Northwest in 1833 for the Hudson's Bay Company, where he was assigned to assist Dr. John McLoughlin in medical practice. He served at Fort Vancouver until 1841 when he returned to Europe for a visit and some post-graduate training in medicine in Paris. Upon return he

was assigned to Fort Nisqually as superintendent of the Nisqually Farms of the Puget Sound Agricultural Company, part of the Hudson's Bay Company operations. He remained at Nisqually until 1859 when he moved to Victoria, following settlement of the claims of the Hudson's Bay Company from the United States, a task in which he played an important role. In Victoria he supervised the Company farms, served as one of the members of the Board of Management of the Company. During all these years of Company service Tolmie studied native language and customs, botany, climbed and explored neighboring mountains, and collaborated on a book on Indian languages. He also served for a time as a member of the legislature of British Columbia. A remarkable figure, he left a permanent impress on northwest history. He died in Victoria in 1886. Mount Tolmie, in Victoria, and Mount Tolmie in the Cascade Range, are named in his honor. (See chapter *Botanizing Scots*.)

49. *Urquhart, James* — Pioneer farmer, town founder, civic leader. Born in Ferentosh, Ross-shire, Scotland, in 1822. At fifteen, he worked in his uncle's general store, then moved to Linlithgow where he worked for the railroad for several years. In 1851 he sailed for New York, then spent several months in the south. In 1852, he joined an emigrant train for Oregon. For a while he performed various jobs: wharf-building at St. Helens, mining in southern Oregon, building a shingle-shaving machine at Oregon City. In 1853, he moved to Cowlitz Landing, where he voted in Washington's first territorial election. After settling on Eden Prairie, he sent for his wife and five children who came from Scotland to join him, their voyage taking six months by way of Cape Horn. Shortly after their arrival, Urquhart purchased and filed on new land near the present site of Napavine, Washington. He laid out the new town in 1883. In addition to farming, Urquhart established a mercantile business, served as county treasurer and postmaster, and was elected to three terms in the territorial legislature. He died in 1901.

50. *Wallace, William* — Territorial Governor, Washington, Representative to Congress; Territorial Governor, Idaho, Representative from Idaho. Born in Troy, Ohio, in 1811, Wallace studied law and practiced in Iowa. He was elected speaker of the House in the first Iowa legislature, and also served as president of the legislative council. He moved to Washington Territory in 1853. He was appointed Governor of Washington Territory by his friend, Abraham Lincoln, in 1861. The same year he resigned to run for the office of Territorial Representative to the U.S. Congress. In 1863, Lincoln again appointed him, this time to be Governor of Idaho Territory. Again, Wallace resigned, and ran for Representative from Idaho. He was present in Washington, D.C. at the time of Lincoln's assassination and served as one of the honorary pallbearers at the funeral in the national capitol. He died in Steilacoom and is buried at Fort Steilacoom, now the grounds of Western State Hospital.

Note: This list could as easily have been expanded to 300 names. It is offered as a sample only of the Scottish contribution. A longer list is being compiled and will be published later as a finding guide.

Acknowledgments

Any book, however small, which covers such a long span of time and a long range of human behavior, means that the author is indebted to many people and institutions for help. It is impossible to list them all here. But it is a happy obligation to name those who have given the most assistance and to thank them for it.

These people and institutions were particularly helpful: Frank Green and Jeanne Engerman, of the Washington State Historical Society library; the staff of Special Collections, University of Washington library; Nancy Pryor, the Northwest Room, Washington State Library; the staff of the Archives of British Columbia; Agnes Conrad, of the State Archives of Hawaii; the staff of the Hawaii Historical Society; the Bancroft Library, University of California; the late David Magee, of San Francisco; the Beinecke Library, Yale University; the Oregon Historical Society; Beaver House, Hudson's Bay Company, London; the National Library of Scotland; the Scottish Record Office; the University of Edinburgh Library; the National Maritime Museum, Greenwich; the London School of Economics of the University of London, and Bernard Crick; the Earl of Galloway, Cumloden, Scotland; the Scottish American Investment Company, Ltd., Edinburgh.

Special thanks are due to Robert Hitchman, for reading the manuscript and offering helpful suggestions; Dr. Clifford M. Drury, for helpful advice on the Oregon Mission; Afton Monson, for patient typing and re-typing; Darrell Thiel, for assistance in reading proof; Kenn Johnson and Alan Bankhead for original art work — Johnson for the map and pioneer portraits, Bankhead for the Scottish crests and portraits.

Finally, I want to express my gratitude to those people of Scottish descent who shared information and, in many cases, pointed me toward other helpful sources: Lucile Metcalf and David Brandon, of the Caledonian Society of Hawaii; Gordon Johnston, former Mayor of Tacoma; Jack Knowles, of Clan Gordon; Harry Padraic Murdock, commissioner of the North Pacific region of Clan Donald; Nancy Rieper, of Tacoma; E. K. Murray and Cecelia Carpenter, descendants of Sir Charles Ross, of the Hudson's Bay Company and Fort Nisqually; Iva Lee Mann, granddaughter of Edward Huggins, the last factor at Fort Nisqually; H. O. Ferguson, of Lac La Hache, British Columbia, great-grandson of Archibald McKinlay, of Fort Walla Walla. There were many others but a blanket thanks must suffice.

None of these informants are responsible for any errors in the book. That credit I reserve for myself, in the hope that criticism will help to unearth new material in this fascinating field for further research.

Ranger, Brest 8th May 1778

Madam

It cannot be too much lamented that in the profession of Arms the Officer of feeling and of real Sensibility should be under the necessity of winking at any Action of Persons under his command which his heart can not approve : but the reflection is doubly severe when he finds himself Obliged in appearance to countenance such Action by his Authority.

This hard case was mine when on the 23d of April last I landed on St Marys Isle. knowing Lord Selkirk's intrest with his King, and esteeming as I do, his private Character, I wished to make him the happy Instrument of alleviating the horrors of hopeless captivity when the brave are overpowered and made Prisoners of War. It was perhaps fortunate for you, Madam, that he was from home; for it was my intention to have taken him on board of Ranger and to have detained him until thro' his means a general and fair Exchange of Prisoners, as well in Europe as in America has been affected .

When I was informed by some Men whom I met at landing that his Lordship was absent, I walked back to my Boat determining to leave the Island : by the way however, some Officers who were with me could not forbear expressing their discontent, observing that in America no delicacy was shown by the English; who took away all sorts of movable property, setting Fire
not

my People, as I determine to punish them if they have exceeded their Liberty.

I have the Honor to be with much esteem and with profound Respect.

Madam

Your most Obedient and most humble Servant.

Jn Paul Jones

The Right Honorable
The Countess of Selkirk
St. Marys Isle
Scotland.

THE

Haughs of Crumdel;

*Giving a full account of that Memorable
Battle fought by the Great Montrose
and the Clans, against Oliver
Cromwell;*

To which are added,

The Broom of Cowdenknowes.
The Highland Plaid.

STIRLING:

Printed and Sold, Wholesale and Retail,
By W. Macnie, Bookseller

1775

120

Tho M'Phersons fought like lions bold,
M,Gregors none could them controul,
M'Lachlan's fought with valiant souls,
   Upon the Haughs of Crumdel.
     Sing, &c.

M'Cleans, M'Dougals, and M'Niels,
So boldly as they took the field,
And made their enemies to yield,
   Upon the Haughs of Crumdel.
     Sing, &c.

The Gordens boldly did advance,
The Frasers fought with sword and lanee,
The Grahams they made their heads to donce,
   Upon the Haughs of Crumdel.
     Sing, &c.

The Royal Stewarts and Monroes,
So boldly as they fac'd their foes,
And brought them down with handly blowrs,
   Upon the Haughs of Crumdel.
     Sing, &c.

Out of twenty thousand Englishmen,
Five hundred fled to Aberdeen,
The rest of them they were all slain,
   Upon the Haughs of Crumdel.
     Sing, &c.

Murdock Coat of Arms

James Christie, Olympic Explorer

Ethnic History Series

General Editor — Bruce Le Roy

The Washington State American Revolution Bicentennial Commission (in cooperation with the Washington State Historical Society and the Northwest Center for American Folklife and Folklore)

with the help of the Donald McFadon Memorial Fund